The Dictionary of Wicca, Witchcraft and Magick

Erik Ravenswood

© 2019 by Erik Ravenswood.

All rights reserved. No part of this book may be reproduced, stored in a retrieval system or transmitted in any form or by any means without the prior written permission of the publishers, except by a reviewer who may quote brief passages in a review to be printed in a newspaper, magazine or journal.

ISBN: 978-1-64713-316-0

Second Edition

Light Of The Moon Publishing has allowed this work to remain exactly as the author intended, verbatim, without editorial input.

Printed in the United States of America

This book is dedicated to my partner in life, who brings light to my life every day.

Table of Contents

Introduction 5

Wiccan, Witchcraft and Magickal Terms 6

Divination Dictionary 85

The Symbolism of Crystals 95

The Symbolism of Birds and Animals 101

The Symbolism of Trees, Plants, and Herbs 107

The Symbolism of Incense and Essential Oils 114

The Symbolism of Colors 119

The Symbolism of Gods and Angels 121

Introduction

I was born a hereditary witch. I come from a family who has practiced witchcraft for more than four generations. Growing up I remember the stories my Great Grandmother told me of Italy and her reading of Tarot Cards and use of a crystal ball for divination.

I was always mesmerized by the aspect of witchcraft but also the need for secrecy. I was raised with the idea that witchcraft was not spoken of in general company, and that bothered me. In the burning times, witches had to hide their practices for fear of life. In today's world, it isn't really that way. Yet we hide who we are and the sharing of knowledge is kind of taboo.

I decided, I wanted to share the experiences I have had with Wicca. I decided my path was a Wiccan one, and also, I am a teacher. I want to share my knowledge and help others who want to learn this path. I am always learning and exploring the history of the craft and feel that whatever I can share might help others along their way as well.

I welcome you to join me on my journey and learn a little more about the vast history or Wicca, Witchcraft and Magick. Included in the book are many different subject areas and full explanations of what they are and how they are used. Please use it as a reference guide in your studies and in everyday life.

I wish you well on your journey, and offer you many blessings.

Wiccan, Witchcraft and Magickal Terms

A

Aboriginal - Pagan tradition explored by the native Australian people.

Abracadabra - Originating from the root name of the Gnostic deity Abraxas with the meaning "hurt me not". It is a Jewish word from the mystical tradition of Qabala. It is said it possesses magickal power, mostly in the form of protection from illness.

Absent Healing - A form of faith healing. The healer is not present and projects positive healing energy from a separate location to the person suffering from illness.

Acolyte - In many magickal orders, it is a person referred to as a "novice" or a person beginning to learn the craft. In every day terms the trainee person in a group.

Adastria - Meaning "inevitable", it is the name applied to the goddess Nemisis. This refers to the goddess's idea of Divine retribution to malicious words, thought or actions.

Adept - An individual who through serious study and accomplishments is highly proficient in a particular magickal way.

Aeromancy - Divination using the stars as reference.

Aes sidhe - Supernatural Folk, i.e. the Faeries.

Afterworld - The afterlife. A place where souls preside after death. See Summerland.

Age of Aquarius - the "New Age" of mankind

Age Of Pisces - On the calendar, there are twelve Zodiac Ages. These ages take their names from the twelve Zodiac Signs inspired by the equinoxes. Based on the Christian calendar, the dates of 400-1999 AD refer to the Piscean Age. The age following is named the Aquarian.

Aicme - Group formed of five Oghams.

Aine - Among the Celtic Goddesses, she who presides is over of crops, the moon and of cattle.

Air - There are four ancient elements known to man. In a magick circle, Air is representative of the East Watchtower in the Northern Hemisphere and the South Watchtower if you are in the Southern Hemisphere. Location to the circle is derivative to hemispheres.

Air Signs - In astrology, Aquarius, Gemini, and Libra are the three signs of the zodiac attributed to the element of Air.

Airbe druad - In magick, it is a barrier that no one may pass through. Basically, a "Hedge".

Airts - In Scottish Gaelic terminology, it means anything that affects the wind. In magick, we cast circles of protection while performing spells. In Scottish Traditional Wicca, when they cast a magickal circle, the four winds would be summoned to guard while a ritual was performed. Basically, Airts, were winds which were identified by the four directions the blew from and the four elements they were a part of. These winds were identified by ruler and colors. The East was ruled by Aes, with the color red, and whose time was dawn. The South was ruled by Deas, with the color white, and the time Noon. The West was ruled by Iar, with the color grey and the time was Dusk. The North was ruled by Tuath with the color black and whose time was Night.

Aisling - pronounced "ash-leen". From Ireland. Meaning a dream or vision. In many stories of Ireland, the person dreaming sees a vision-woman or speir-bhean. It is said this figure is from other worlds or possible from the dead.

Aka - A "Silver Cord" possibly from biblical reference. It connects the body to the soul. The cord between the Physical body and the astral body.

Akasha - In magick and the occult, it is the fifth element. Referred to as "Otherworld" or the "Spiritual Ether".

Akasha Spirit - Related to the fifth element, it refers to the omnipresent power that is woven throughout the whole universe.

Akashic Records - According to Edward Cayce, there is somewhere out there a record of all past lives, healing, magick and spirituality. It is believed to exist on a psychic plane and not on the physical one. It is said to be accessible by astral travel, or possible visualization into one's mind.

Alba - The Isle of Skye, Scotland

Alban Arthuan - Winter Solstice.

Alban Eiler - Spring Equinox.

Alban Elved - Autumnal Equinox.

Alban Heruin - Summer Solstice.

Alchemist - One who practices the art of alchemy.

Alchemy - Originating from the Middle Ages, Alchemy is a form of high magick noted by the attempts of alchemists to turn lead into gold.

Aleuromancy - A form of Divination. In this process, answers are written on paper and baked into dough balls. There is a direct relation to modern fortune cookies.

Alexandrian Tradition - Developed by Alex and Maxine Sanders in the 1960s in Britain, it is a form of Garderian Wicca.

Alexandrian Witches - Founded independently in the 1960's by Alex and Maxine Saunders, an offshoot of Gardnerian witchcraft.

Alignment - A balancing in the chakras of the body. This is often achieved by a synchronization of mental and spiritual vibrations in tune with a specific god, goddess, or spiritual body.

Allegory - Thought of as a supreme achievement in the Pagan Religion. Allegory is the use of understandable symbols to explain a difficult or abstract concept.

All Hallows Eve - A Pagan festival and another name for Samhain. It is a Sabbat which is celebrated on the last day of April and the first day of May in the Southern Hemisphere and the last day of October and first day of November in the Northern Hemisphere.

Altar - A personal place where magick is created. A special table or place where ritual items are placed for work and worship. It can be created from any material, from marble to simply a patch of earth. Traditionally items included on an alter can include but are not limited to, candles, an athame, a wand, water, salt, stones, incense and statues. Alters are generally made of wood and stone. Metal is not a good choice because of its conductivity. Metal can however be used to adorn and make decorations.

Altar Cloth - A cloth used to decorate an alter space. The history of the cloth dictates that it originated in a time that cloth was hand woven and many times embroidered with a symbol to acknowledge a special occasion such as a Sabbat. In many alters, the alter cloth is matched to a wall hanging used behind the alter. In any case it is a connection between the alter and the user and a sign of their magickal connection.

Altar Table - A personal place where magick is created. A special table or place where ritual items are placed for work and worship. It can be created from any material, from marble to simply a patch of earth. Traditionally items included on an alter can include but are not limited to, candles, an athame, a wand, water, salt, stones, incense and statues. Alters are generally made of wood and stone. Metal is not a good choice because of its conductivity. Metal can however be used to adorn and make decorations.

Amulet - An item that is charged with person's energy through a ritual or meditation. It is used to protect or ward off people or evil.

Ancestors - Ancestors are our past. Our families, and those who shaped our lives and allowed us to become who we are. This term is most commonly used as a deceased family member. Ancestors are not necessarily someone you are related to by blood. They can someone who has gone before us in a coven or grouping or someone we particularly admire.

Ancestors are also persons we are drawn to and are spirits we honor for inspiring us to become who we are. They might be someone who we have developed a psychic bond with. In some cases they act as Spirit Guides to us, guiding us as we go through life. To strengthen the bond, Ancestors should be acknowledged and honored regularly.

An-da-shealladh - In simple terms, "two sights" it is thought of as the ability to see spirits.

Anima - In a man's psyche, they are the buried feminine elements.

Animism - A belief that natural objects, or possibly Nature itself, are alive and have a consciousness.

Animistic - The belief that all forms of Nature have a Divine Spirit attached to them.

Animus - In a woman's psyche, they are the buried masculine elements.

Ankh - The symbol of life in Egyptian hieroglyphics, also a sign of love, and reincarnation. It is the form of a cross with a looped top.

Annwyn - Pronounced (ar-ahn) it is the Under World.

An-Shet - Another word for a Wiccan or Witch's magickal wand.

Aphorism - A thinly worded saying. An example would be: "As above, So below."

Aphrodisiac - Substance or concoction that generates sexual arousal.

Apparition - The appearance of a ghost or the like often seen in a dream, trance or waking state, possibly the result of astral projection.

Aquarius - The 11th sign in the zodiac. Its symbol is the Water Bearer, and is an Air sign. It is ruled by Uranus.

Aradia - The Italian Goddess Diana's daughter, and a name for the Goddess used by Italian witches or Strega. She is said to be the origin of all witches and sworn to protect her people against the evils of man. She taught around 1353, and was imprisoned more than once. She escaped several times and eventually disappeared into history.

Arcana - Represents the two halves of the tarot deck. The major Arcana consists of 22 cards, each representing larger possible events in life. The minor arcana consists of 56 suit cards (also called the lesser arcana) representing the minor events in life and supporting the major Arcana.

Archetype - The symbols and imagery in visions, dreams, meditation and of the mind. They are used to interpret the meanings of dreams and help us to better communicate with our subconscious.

Arianhod - A Welsh Goddess whose name means 'Silver Wheel'. When used as Caer Arianrhod (Castle of Arianrhod), it refers to the resting place of a soul in its wait for reincarnation.

Aries - The 1st sign of the zodiac. Symbolized by the Ram, it is a Fire sign, and ruled by Mars.

Aromatherapy - It is used therapeutically to heal, relax, and purify. The process uses flowers, herbs, oils or anything that has scent.

Arthurian Tradition - A Welsh version of paganism based on the history of King Arthur, Merlin the Sorcerer, and Guinevere.

As Above So Below - The ancient maxim "As Above, So Below" is ultimately based on the same principle as all forms of divination. It is attributed to the Egyptian spiritual Master Hermes Trismegistus. Basically, it means that being it great or small, we are all a part of the Divine Nature or plan. All things are based on the divine God and Goddess and all things reflect their qualities. For this reason, if you are open to the belief, the same truth can be found in the great and the small.

Arthurian Tradition - A Welsh paganism based on the story of King Arthur, Merlin the Sorcerer, and Guinevere.

Asatru - Modern worship of the old Norse gods.

Aspect - Around us is a Creative Life Force. Aspect is the principle or part of it that is worked with at any given time.

Aspecting - Referring to magickal practice where a practitioner attempts to acquire a aspect of a God or Goddess. This is usually done in a coven and not by a solitary witch. As seen with the pagan ritual of Drawing Down The Moon, or in Vodou, it is where a Priest or Priestess allows a Deity to speak through them using their body.

Asperger - A bundle of fresh herbs used to sprinkle the water during ritual purification. They usually carry dew or are dowsed with spring water.

Asperging - During or preceding Ritual, it is the act of sprinkling water for purification and cleansing.

Astral - Another dimension of reality.

Astral Body - The psychic copy of creation in the physical body. It consists of substance weaker than matter, but stronger than mind or spirit. (See also Etheric.)

Astral Plane - A plane that is parallel to the physical world, it is traveled through during astral projection.

Astral Projection/Travel - Separating your astral body from your physical body, to project yourself in travel through the astral.

Astrology - The practice of interpreting the arrangement of stars and planets in relation to astrological zodiacs. Thus, revealing possible future events.

Ategenos - A rebirth after death and experiencing the Other World.

Athame - A Wiccan ritual knife. It is almost never used for cutting and need not be sharpened. It is not used to draw blood. Wiccan's never use blood or animals in any rituals. It is primarily used to direct power or energy. It is like a wand but used in different common ways. (See Boline and Wand)

Attune - The act of bringing different psyches into harmony.

Augury - Divination based on "signs" or omens.

Aura - An energy field which surrounds all living beings. Not everyone can see an aura. It is a gift at birth to some and a trained ability to others. The aura when visible contains many colors that dictate spiritual and emotional elements of humans and things that influence it by surroundings. Auras can be heard, felt or sensed by other methods.

Automatic Writing - Form of divination where a person with the ability to channel enters an altered state, and uses a pen and paper to receive messages.

Autumn Equinox - One of the eight Sabbats celebrated on the middle of Autumn. Also known as: Alban Elfed, Mabon and the Second Festival of Harvest.

Avatar - A soul that is advanced in intelligence and skills, who returns to a physical form to teach less evolved souls. Examples: Buddha, Jesus.

Awen - Inspiration.

Awenyddion - Inspired ones.

B

Balefire - A fire ignited for magical or religious purposes. Much like a bonfire and used outdoors.

Bane - Anything that is harmful, destructive or evil.

Banish - To remove an entity or exorcise something by use of magick. The rid the presence of.

Banishing - 1. In Magick, a circle is created for the purpose of protection. When finished with a spell and the ritual is over the circle is banished. 2. Banishing of an individual includes removal from a coven or group for a possible inexcusable offense or breaking of core rules such as harm no one. 3. An entity that is harmful can be banished, possibly one in the form of a ghost or spirit, for protection.

Banishing Ritual - A ritual which is performed to remove negative or dark forces influences from a circle.

B.C.E - Before Common Era, non-Christian version of B.C.

Beithe Luis Nion - An Old name from the Irish for the Celtic Tree Ogham.

Bellarmine Jars - A large jar said to have been decorated with the face of Cardinal Bellarmine. In many cases the jar had three faces on it, all of the same man. In some cases, the faces were conjoined. Some believed the face on the jars represented the Horned God. These jars were popular for magickal uses.

Bells - Bells are often used in rituals. They are thought to invoke directional energies. In ritual, they are used to ring in Sabbats and scare away baneful spirits.

Beltane - Pronounced "Bal-tene". The traditional Sabbat where the rule of the "Wheel of the Year" is given back to the Goddess. On this night great bonfires are built and cattle are driven in between to protect them from disease. Couples wishing fertility are encouraged to jump fires on Beltane nights. Celebrated in festivals beginning May First in the Northern Hemisphere. Other names for the festival include: Bealtiunn, Shenn da Boaldyn, and Galan-Mai.

Beo - Refers to life, or living. It can also mean quick, alive, active, lively. It can also mean transformed by external magick by others or in shape-shifted into a true form.

Besom - In simple terms a witch's broomstick. It is a bundle of twigs tied to a handle that is used to cleanse or purify and place.

Bibliomancy - A form of divination. In this, you let a book fall open, and without looking, you point to a specific spot on the open page. This passage or word is meant to inspire you to find an answer to a question or situation.

Bi-Location - Similar to Astral Projection, but in this case, you remain aware of your bodies current surroundings.

Bind - To stop, prevent or limit a person, place or thing. In magick, it is the equivalent of casting a Binding Spell. In this case it is not to harm anyone, but to protect others from harm. In Wicca / Witchcraft, this act is thought to be unethical.

Binding - Restraining a person place or thing and preventing their use of power to harm others or restraining a spell.

Bindrunes - Made of metal or wood, it is a powerful talisman that is inscribed with two or more runes.

Bith - The world where we live, the visible multi-verse.

Black Mirror - A tool sometimes used for divination and in some cases dark practices.

Blath - Prosperity. The eastern realm among the Fifths.

Blessed Be - A simple blessing meaning hello or goodbye. It is commonly used by Wiccans and Pagans. It is derived from the ritual of the Five-fold Kiss.

Blood of the Moon - A woman's monthly menstrual cycle. A time when magick is to be performed and in conjunction with a full moon is quite powerful.

Bodhisattva - A human entity that has evolved to an extremely high plane of existence. It no longer needs to be reincarnated into human form, but chooses to, in order to help man.

Bodhran - From Ireland meaning "Cow-song"; A single-head frame drum.

Boline; Boleen - A Wiccan ritual knife. It is used for more practical purposes, such as cutting herbs. Generally white handled with a curved blade. It is usually quite dull and never used for the purposes or drawing blood or killing. It is used for various magickal operations, notably casting the Magick Circle, and to create magickal artifacts. It is normally only used within the circle.

Book of Shadows - A book used by Wiccans and Witches to collect spells, recipes, journal entries, magick, advice, and coven laws among other things. It can be a collective of a coven or just for use by a solitary practitioner. Also known as a Witch's

Grimoire. This is basically a collection of information for reference. The name is believed to be a remainder from the burning times when witches had to remain "in the shadows".

There is no one individual Book Of Shadows. Each is written by the owner of the book. It may contain information copied from a coven's B.O.S., or it has been tradition for students to copy their teachers book. The idea is that you copy information in your "own hand of write" (own handwriting). It is acceptable that you copy information from another adept Witch.

By tradition when a Witch or Wiccan dies, their Book Of Shadows is destroyed unless otherwise instructed to hand the book down to a sibling or give it over to their coven. In most cases the coven disposes of the book.

Book Religions - Religion is split into two concepts Native (or Pagan) religions, and the Book religions. In Pagan religion, people beliefs grow out of their belief in Gods and Deity. It is a belief in nature and the metaphysical. Belief grows and changes as culture and abilities develop. In Book religion beliefs descend from the Bible and Koran. They are believed to perfect in origin and must never change or evolve.

Boomerang Effect - A principle that applies the three-fold law. If a person launches a psychic attack on someone with stronger powers, the repercussions will come back three-fold.

Born Old - Being born old refers to a person who is born with such a thin veil between conscious and powers of the soul that they can access their higher self easily with minimal effort and no instruction. They are said to be "born old". They are born with talents that take others a lifetime to master. It is believed these individuals had put forth great effort to master their skills in previous lives, and bring them into the present.

Breaca sith - "faerie marks," the discolored spots that appear on the face of one who is dying.

Brehon Laws - Old Irish laws governing all aspects of life.

Bri - It is the power of creative intent that defines you. It is your Strength, energy, vigor, merit, essence, and natural talent. This power can be limited. It is within all people, places and objects. See Bua.

Bricht - The spoken spell. Anything Magickal.

Brigid - The triple aspect goddess: Maiden, Mother and Crone.

Broom Closet - A person who is not public about their magickal or Pagan practices or beliefs. They are described as "in the broom closet".

Bruho/Bruha - The Spanish word for "witch". In this term, it is a reference to a bad witch. See "curranderismo" for good witch.

Bua - A power that is developed from ritual, blessings and sanctification. The power is a limited one. It can be shared with others, stored, increased or decreased. It includes areas of success, skill, talent, destiny and victory. See Bri.

Buabhaill - Drinking horn.

Burning Times - The burning times is a name used to describe a point in history when witches were executed for their beliefs. These persecutions took place from the Middle Ages onward (circa 1000 C.E. through the 17th century). Although historical accounts describe there being thousands, or possible more witches killed, most of these were not actually witches. Many were Christians or heretics accused of witchcraft simply as a way to get rid of them.

While the description is misleading, most were hanged and not burned.

Burrin - A name for the White Handled Knife.

Bwa'r Crach - Referred to as "hag's bow," it is the rainbow leading to the Other World.

C

Cabala - See Qabala. The ancient Hebrew system of Magick.

Caer - A Castle or fortress.

Cakes And Ale - The meal shared with the God or Goddess at the end of a religious ritual. This meal consists of cakes which can be biscuits or crackers or specially baked breads. It is often served with ale which can be an alcoholic beverage or juice, water, milk or other beverages. The food and drinks are blessed before consumption. A portion of the ale is left for libation. The whole ceremony is similar to Communion and is a time to give thanks and remember what we have been given.

Call - Invoking divine forces.

Cancer - The 4th sign in the zodiac. Symbolized by the Crab, it is a Water sign, and is ruled by the Moon.

Candle Magick - A form of magick that uses different colored candles as instruments of magick. The colors are used as directional tools to focus the energy towards a person or the intent desired. The candle and color are used to focus your energy. The candle is lit and focused on during meditation. The candle may be allowed to burned out or extinguished when done. As the candle burns the desired outcome is believed to be achieved. Sometimes, the candle may be relit over several days to accomplish the desired goal.

Candlemas - Pagan Sabbat held on Feb. 1.

Capricorn - The 10th sign of the zodiac. It is symbolized by the Goat, is an Earth sign, and is ruled by the Saturn.

Cantripa - A small spell cast by a witch that is quick and has minimal effects.

Cardinal Points - The four elements defined by the directions of North, East, South, and West. Symbolized by the circle in magic (which connects the points), and the watchtowers.

Casting Cloth - A layout cloth marked with appropriate symbols for casting runes or tossing the Ogham Fews.

Cath - Meaning Conflict: The northern realm among the Fifths.

Catharsis - At the height of a ritual, it is the release of magickal energies.

Cauldron - A symbol life, death, rebirth and the goddess. It is most associated with Cerridwen, who brewed a magickal cauldron from which a single drop was yielded each year. It is said that wisdom was granted to the one who received her brew. It is said that the cauldron not only is represented in pagan ritual but also in the Christian concept of the holy grail.

C.E. - Common Era. Synonymous with A.D. but without religious bias.

Celtic - A mystical people believed to have developed in Central or Eastern Europe around 700 BCE and spread through Western Europe. The Celts developed a distinctive and highly mystical culture. They are believed to be a major contributor to modern Wiccan thought. The Greek philosopher Pythagoras cited the Druids as a source for many of his teachings as well.

Censer - A container in which incense can be smoldered or burned. It is symbolized by the element of air. It is also used during a ritual to purify and is worked in a circle to generate its power.

Centering - Used with meditation it is the process of grounding your energy. It is also used to harness and balance your energy.

Ceremonial Magick - Based on Kabala, a highly codified magickal tradition.

Cerne Abbas - Believed to represent the Horned God, the Cerne Abbas Giant is a huge chalk carving in the English countryside. It is a carving of a naked man with a huge erect penis. "Cerne" is believed to be a shortened form of "Cernunnos."

Cernunnos - The Horned God - With the facet of the god but depicted by a man with antlers and sometimes the tail and legs of a stag. He is often pictured sitting cross-legged with a torch in one hand and a serpent in the other.

Cerridwen - The Celtic grain goddess.

Chakras - The seven major energy vortexes in the human body. Each associated with a color and sound. These vortexes are: crown-violet, forehead-indigo, throat-blue, chest-green, naval-yellow, abdomen-orange, groin- red.

Challenge - The process that tests courage before the initiation into witchcraft.

Chalice - A symbol for the element of water. It is used during rituals and the contents are blessed and passed around to members of the coven so everyone may bring the Goddess into themselves. Represented as a feminine symbol.

Channeling - Also called Mediumship; it is a process where an entity speaks through a human.

Chant - Used in meditation and spell-casting, it is repeatedly saying lines, phrases or words over and over again to achieve a desired effect.

Chaos - Unity or Union. The original state or point of creation. The beginning and the end of a given form but existing in a dreamlike state. A mix of male and female, dark and light all mixed together at once. Also a God or Goddess before creation primordial.

Chaote - A Chaos practitioner not actively using their skill.

Chaplet - Flowers woven into a crown for the head worn at Beltane.

Charge - The Story of the Goddess to her children. Written by Doreen Valiente.

Charge, The - The traditional Garderian/Alexandrian declaration by the High Priestess in the name of the Goddess.

Charging - Charging and object with your own power. Traditionally done with stones, and magickal objects.

Charles Godfrey Leland - Student of Witchcraft and a folklorist, Vangelo Delle Streghe.

Charms - An item be it amulet or talisman that has been infused with a witches power. Mostly used to enchant or bring pleasure, it can also protect from harm. Energy in a charm can be instilled for a specific purpose.

Cheiromancy - A form of divination based on reading of the hand, similar to palmistry.

Chi - From the Chinese, meaning the total universal life force.

Chinese Elements - fire, earth, metal, water and wood.

Circle, Magic - In Wicca and Witchcraft, it is the sphere of energy created to protect while magick is practiced. Just as the circle is created to perform magick, at the end it is deconstructed. The ground within is considered sacred and a place where one might meet a deity. Methods of creation vary greatly, but in most cases, they involve an athame, salt, and water.

Circle of Protection; COP - See Circle.

Cleansing - Traditionally performed before rituals, it involves a cleanse of the body and mind. The body by a bath often containing salt to purify. And the mind through meditation.

Coelbreni - Sticks for divination.

Coiced - One of five provinces of the land or cosmos.

Coirc - A magick cauldron used in creation of potions and casting spells.

Collective Unconsciousness - All living things past and present have a connection. This sentient connection is a collective unconsciousness.

Coming of Age Ritual - A pagan ritual for coming of age in boys and girls. With girls it happens with their first menses. With boys when they achieve the age of 13. It is at this point they become spiritual adults. It is also the age they are permitted into covens.

Cone of Power - A gathering of psychic energy either by an individual or group and released to perform a certain task.

Conjure - To call forth spirits from the spirit realm into the physical plane.

Conscious Mind - The part of our mind that is aware of our surroundings. We use it when we perform everyday tasks. It is the rational half of our consciousness.

Consecration - In Magick, it is the cleansing or charging of an object to be used to cast spells, or other magickal uses. Items can be blessed and dedicated to a deity.

COP; Circle of Protection - See Circle.

Corn Dolly - A symbol of fertility and grain, it is like a poppet made of wheat. It celebrates aspects of the Goddess.

Corp creidh - Meaning "clay body," it is sculpted clay used as a poppet in magick.

Correspondences - The use of items in Magick which are related to a specific goal. A colored candle can be used to cast a specific spell. Green candles represent prosperity and would be used in a specific spell. Specific stones have their own properties that can power spells. Other items that can be used are herbs, incense, numbers, stones and many others.

Correspondence is also a teaching system. In this, teaching, they use the idea of Sympathy, which says items that have similar properties may represent one another. So the Element of Air would correspond with that direction.

Coven - A group of witches who form a group to practice witchcraft. Often limited to 13 members, they traditionally are smaller in group size. The group is led by a High Priest or High Priestess.

Covenstead - The meeting place of a particular coven.

Cowan - In terms of a Wiccan or Witch, it is a non- Wiccan Or Witch. It is similar to the way a Jewish person would refer to a gentile as not being Jewish. It is generally used as a derogatory word for a pagan who is considered a poser.

Craebh Ciuil - Meaning "the silver branch," or faerie shaman's magick wand.

Craft, the - A term used to refer to Witchcraft and Wicca.

Crane Bag - A Shaman's bag which holds magickal talismans, stones, crystals and totems. Also associated with an Air Witch.

Crannchur - Meaning "casting the woods," or divining by oghams.

Crone - Symbolized by the waning moon, the cauldron, the carrion crow and the color black. It is a term used for a witch who is over 50-56 years old. Usually meaning she has passed menopause. She is represented by the Sabbats of Mabon and Samhain.

The Crone is said to rule over wisdom, understanding, magick, death, regeneration and learning, among other things. She (Crone Goddess) is thought of as the "Goddess of Death" and is often feared. It is said she consumes all things, but is said to give them transformation and rebirth.

In present day the crone is most associated with Halloween. The pointed hat is associated with an upward spiraling cone of power, her broomstick for sweeping away the old, and her cauldron for creating new creations.

Croning - The rite of passage from Witch to Crone.

Cross of Confusion - An Ancient Roman symbol which questioned the validity of Christianity.

Cross Quarter Days - In the wheel of the year, there are four fire Sabbats (Samhain, Imbolb, Beltane, Lammas). The festivals for these Sabbats form a cross on the wheel.

Crystallomancy - Divination using crystals

Cunning Man - A term older than Christianity. He was the bringer of Magick. He was relied on by villager to ensure a good harvest and to protect from evil forces. He provided magickal charms and medicines. With the rise of Christianity, the Cunning Man disappeared.

Curse - The purposeful use of directing negative energy towards a person place or thing.

Cwn Annwn - (pronounced COON-ANOON) Often referred to as Hell Hounds, they are the hunting dogs of the faeries.

Cybele - The Phrygian version of the Great Mother. She was adopted by the Romans as the Mother of all Gods. It was taught that Cybele was the first being in existence in the universe.

D

Daemon - A Greek word meaning spirit.

Dark Half - A process of looking inward. In the process, the goal is to attain a tight focus. It is the process of Involution. Examples: The night is the dark half of the day. Winter is the dark half of a year.

Days of Power - Certain days of the year contain more magickal power than others. These days are usually based around Sabbats. See also Sabbats.

Dedication - Accepting the Craft as a way of life and vowing to learn its history, lore and become an adept.

Degree - Attaining a level of status as a practitioner. In magickal studies, you must pass various tests of knowledge and experience in order to climb to the next level in your tradition.

In the Wiccan system, there are three degrees. A Novice is a new seeker who wishes to achieve the First-Degree Initiation. This consists of a year and one day of study. After they are entitled to call themselves Priest or Priestess. From then they can progress through Second Degree and then to Third Degree. A Third-Degree Witch is entitled to teach and have his or her own coven. It is done differently depending on the coven.

Deity - A god or goddess. Often thought of as immortal, they are a divine aspect of creation. Beyond human form, they are deemed immortal. Different religions are represented by different god & goddess names, or different deities. These make up the Pantheon of that religion. Each deity has their own abilities and powers.

Deosil - Deosil refers to motions that go in the same direction as the motion of the Sun. Moving clockwise in movement and ritual. The opposite is Widdershins. Deosil movement brings spiritual energy into physical materialization. It literally means "Southwards".

Raising of energy is necessary in the creation of magick. It is energy that allows us to manifest the things we wish to bring about. Deosil allows the raising of energy needed to cast spells. For this reason, most motion in casting a Magick Circle will be Deosil.

Destiny - Ultimately the lessons afforded to a person in life. They give us a chance for growth and advancement. What we do with these lessons is our own choice and can bring about both positive and negative experiences in life. The lessons are given prior to birth to stimulate development of the soul. In can be thought of as a preordained life chosen before birth and cannot be changed. Opportunities are the result of our own choices and actions.

Dirk - Ritual knife in the Scottish tradition.

Divination - The art of seeing the future or the unknown by interpreting signs, symbols or patterns. Often mislabeled as fortune telling, it includes such areas as rune stones, scrying, tarot cards, I Ching and others. It is thought of the art of using the Collective Unconsciousness to seek information. This can be from people, places, events past and present.

Divine Power - Power wielded and used by the God and Goddess. The Life Force. The Ultimate source of all life.

Do As You Will, But Harm Ye None - The golden rule of Wicca. The Wiccan Rede. Basically, what you send out come back to you. A belief that only constructive actions and magick should be sent out into the world. If you use your actions to harm another, it will bring you harm in the end.

Doctrine of Signatures - A belief that herbs, plants and flowers have a unique quality, vibration or energy of their own.

Dogma - A set of believes that are meant to be accepted without question. These beliefs are very rigid and cannot be challenged. In Wicca, there are no such beliefs. Anything in Wicca is open to debate or interpretation. Wiccans have a right to believe what they wish within the framework of what feels right to them.

Dowsing - Using a stick or rod to locate something. Usually a person or place, it can also be an object. This process can also be used for simple yes and no questions.

Dracomancer - Using Dragons in the practice of magick.

Drake - Used in referring to a young dragon.

Drawing Down the Moon - An Ancient Pagan ritual to gather the power of the moon. It is often performed on Esbats. It is mainly used to empower one's self and unite with a particular deity.

Drawing Down the Sun - A very seldom used ritual where the essence of the Sun God is drawn into a male witch's body. Similar to the ritual of Drawing Down The Moon, but not as widely used.

Dreamtime - Shamanistic concept that believes there is a world that parallels this one.

Druid - A person of the Celtic Mystical Order

Druidism - Related to Neo-Paganism, it is a ancient Celtic Order of Priests.

Dryw - Wren, or druid.

Duality - Two opposites in polarity. In religion it could be the difference in good and evil separated into two god like forms.

Duile - The Elements. The list may include: earth, water, stone, salt, sun, rain, cloud, stars and wind. It can also include things such as: an entity, creature, affection, hope, desire, fondness. It can also reflect how we interact with life and deal with situations. Sometimes there are seven or nine duile in a Faerie Pagan's worldview.

E

Earthing - See Grounding.

Earth Magick - Magick that involves the Earth and Earth Energies. All power is drawn from Mother Earth (or Gaia) and elements of earth rituals.

Earth Plane - The world we live in. Another name for your everyday state of consciousness.

Earth Power - The force or energy that exists in inanimate objects such as stones, crystals, metals, fire, and plants. These items can be used and controlled in magick.

Eclectic - A person who blends ideas and traditions to make their own unique style of Wicca, Witchcraft or Paganism that works for them.

Elder - An accomplished figure in a group or organization. Someone who is experienced and older who oversee the operations of a church and its functions. These people have usually gained their title by experience, education, adeptship and accomplishments.

Elemental - A spirit with the energy or power of one of the five elements. The 5 elementals are salamanders (fire), sylphs (air), undines (water), gnomes (earth), and spirit (Akasha).

Elements - The four states of elements are: Earth, Air, Fire and Water. In Witchcraft a fifth element is added with spirit or Akasha.

Each of these elements has a direction in a magickal circle: Earth=north

Air=east
Fire=south
Water=west
Akasha=center

These elements are all vital to sustain life and are found within each individual.

Eleven - Secretive tradition which works closely with elemental beings.

Elixir - A liquid charged with magick that has to have a crystal in it for a given amount of time to be ready to drink.

Elizabethan Age - The age of intellectual growth and Renaissance. It was this period that lead to persecution of witches and sympathizers.

Empower - To transfer energy to a person or object.

Empowerment - Related to spiritual, physical, mental, and magickal. It is a person's assertion of power, energy, or strength in all fields.

Enchantment - A spell cast to gain control over another thing or have authority over it. The spell usually involves spoken words of power. Also used are enchanted objects that continue to affect the person who carries the item.

Eostre's Eggs - Named for the Teutonic Goddess Eostre, they are colored eggs used for celebration purposes.

Esbat - Commonly held on full moons in honor of the goddess, it is any Wiccan celebration which is not a Sabbat.

Essential Oil - A plant oil that is used in rituals. Usually very expensive, the process to remove the oil from a plant doesn't yield much oil. The substance yielded by plants is rarely in oil form but is still called oil.

Evocation - The act of calling something out from within.

Evoking - The act of summoning a non-material entity usually of a lower nature than a human.

Evolution - In Involution, the process involves going inside yourself. A narrowing of one's views to an individual level. In Evolution, the opposite is true. It involves coming out of the individual person and moving towards the Divine. In the process, vibration increases and lightens density making the human form less physical. This is the process of returning to Goddess and to a perspective universality.

Exorcism - A Process that expels demons from a possessed body.

F

Faerie - See Elemental

Faerie Burgh - An Earthen mound where a Faerie colony has its underground home.

Fairy Ring - A powerful place where Wiccans and Witches perform spells.

Familiar - In magick, a familiar is a spirit or guardian the is tied to a human being and a companion in magick. This spirit is often linked to a possession or animal. This is often related to Witches and their having black cats. These cats are not necessarily always familiars. They are magickal creatures and often a familiar.

Fascination - The act of taking control of another person's mind. In Wicca, this process is not acceptable and is in violation of the Rede. This process is considered very manipulative and controlling.

Fate - The guided path in life with a sequence of preplanned events.

Feng Shui - The ancient Chinese art that involves Geomancy based on directions and the five elements. The idea is based on allowing free flow of spiritual energy. The concept is to create a more harmonious and productive space. In the end it is believed it will attract love and success. In many cases, it is used to align positions of building and items within a room.

Fetch - An assistant to a coven's High Priestess. Also called an Summoner, this individual is usually a male.

Fey - Faerie folk.

Fith-Fath - Also called a poppet or a dolly, it is an enchantment that can be used to obtain an affect.

Five-fold Kiss - A Salute usually issued between a High Priestess and A High Priest.

Folklore - Information including sayings, medicines, cures, folk wisdom and other things from a particular local which is separate from mythology.

Folk Magick - The use of crystals, and herbs to project personal power and energy and bring about needed changes.

Freefalling - Allowing changes to occur at random.

Full Moon - The Phase of the moon when it is fully waxed. It is a time of high power when casting spells and using magick in general.

Futhark - (Germanic) Originating from the Norse, it is a form of divination involving the Runic alphabet. It is divided into two, being the elder Futhark and the younger Futhark with fewer Runes.

G

Gaea/Gaia - The spirit of Mother Earth.

Gardnerian Tradition - Based on Gerald Gardener, it is the tradition of witchcraft based on his teachings. Gardener was the founder of modern Wicca. Today many covens have expanded and built on these ideas.

Garter - The Garter is used by Wiccan High Priestesses (and less often by High Priests) as a symbol of rank. A band of cloth, leather, or metal, worn around the leg just above or below the knee, or on the arm just above the elbow, the Garter is an ancient garment still in use as an item of dress. There are many variations on exactly how a Garter should be made.

Geas - Basically, it is something that is one's destiny. Your planned future. From an old witch's term for something like "the raven that sits and whispers on my shoulder."

Geomancy - The art of studying the Earth's energies and aligning ourselves to harness and use these to our best advantage. Aligning ourselves adds effectiveness to our workings.

Glamour - A Magickal illusion used to disguise and change people's immediate perception of you. The change is temporary and can mean things such as changing eye color, hair length, height and others. The process lasts only as long as a witch feeds energy into it.

Glyph - A sigil (symbol) imbued with magick.

Gnome - An elemental that dwells in the earth plane. See Elementals.

God - A term used to refer to a male deity. Some of his names include: Herne, Zeus, Apollo, Odin and others. He is sometimes referred to as the horned god and not to be confused with Satan. His horns are deer antlers to symbolize the Lord of the Hunt. Horns on a God have long been used as a symbol of power. In Christianity, horns were put on their devil as a way to tie him to the horned god and spread misinformation about witchcraft.

Goddess - The female deity. Her names include Aradia, Gaea, Isis, Brigid, Diana, Kali, Lakshmi, Hecate and others. She is symbolic in phases of the moon, such as: Maiden (waxing), Mother (full), and Crone (waning).

Godhead - Known in many different languages and cultures, it is the great over-soul of the known Universe. The over-soul is divided into male & female components: The God & Goddess. The Godhead is the soul of nature. Nature is the body of the Godhead.

Gods - Often referred to as deities, they are immortal beings. They are worshipped by their followers and invoked for magick. A god is generally thought as male.

God Voice - Building of force and then issuing a tone form deep within.

Grammary - Magick in its written form including words, symbols, signs, Oghams and sigils.

Great Rite - This rite marks the initiation into the third degree. It is sexual, but can be performed symbolically instead.

Great Year - The twelve Zodiacal Ages in a complete circle, from one sign back to itself again, also referred to as a Great Year. This is a period of 19,200 years.

Green Man - Another name for God.

Gregorian Calendar - A new calendar introduced in 1582 by Pope Gregory X111. This new calendar replaced the older Julian one. This calendar was based on the birth of Jesus Christ, and divides time into two halves based on that date. Pre-Christian dates count backwards. This makes Jesus appear to be the center of time.

Grimoire - Similar to a book of shadows, it is a magickal workbook that is used to store information about rituals, spells, history, correspondences, and tools.

Gris-Gris - In African religious systems, it is a charm, fetish, or amulet.

Grounding - A process of returning energy back to the God or the Goddess from which it came. This process involves clearing and releasing the energy and helps us to feel calm. This is traditionally done before and after a magickal ritual.

Guardians - Referred to as the guardians of the watchtowers or guardians of the four quarters.

H

Hag Stone/Holey Stone - A Stone with a hole through it that is used to protect against negative forces. It is usually worn around the neck on a red thread. This stone can also be used to bring good luck and fortune to the wearer.

Hallows, Halloween - Halloween is a celebration observed on October 13st. It is on the eve of Samhain. It is on October 13st in the Northern Hemisphere, and on May 1st in the Southern Hemisphere.

Handfasting - The joining of two humans in a bond of love before the God and Goddess. In the ceremony, the two have their hands bound as a symbol of their union as one. In this ceremony, it can be a legal union. Marriages do not have to be Christian to be accepted in most countries.

Handparting - Just like a divorce. It is a separation of what has been joined together. It symbolically cuts the bonds created by a handfasting.

Haruspicy- Divination by animal entrails.

Heathen - There are several definitions for this, among them are: **1.** Someone who does not recognize the God of the Bible. **2.** A pagan. **3.** An irreligious, uncivilized person. Can be used in this context as a negative term for a pagan.

Hecate - Patron of magick and of wisdom, she was the great Crone Goddess of ancient Greece and a Goddess of the Spirit world.

Hedge Witch - A witch who follows the path of a shaman, a solitaire.

Hedge Wizard - A rural practitioner with little formal training, or none at all.

Heptagram - Symbolic of the number seven, it is a seven-pointed star drawn with an unbroken line. In reference to the seven traditional astrological planets but also to the seven planes and sub planes and the seven chakras.

Herbalism - Art of using herbs to assist human needs both magickally and medicinally.

Hereditary Witch - The name used by witches who claim their practices have been continuous in the family. See also Traditional.

Herne The Hunter - A ghost or apparition said to appear in Windsor Great Park, along with his hounds. Pagans recognize him as the ancient Horned God. Seeing Herne is considered an omen of death, which is not surprising since the Horned God was always connected with death and winter. "Herne" is believed to be a shortened form of "Cernunnos."

Hexagram - A Six-pointed star that is formed by putting together two equilateral triangles. It represents the belief of " As above, so below" which is representative of the harmony between the Macrocosm and the Microcosm.

Hierophant - A priest or master of the mysteries who reveals his secrets only to his initiate.

High Magick - Ceremonial magick involving the actions of deities or spirits.

High Priest - Within a coven, a male witch, who has been initiated into the 3rd degree. Abbreviated in written rituals as HP.

High Priestess - Within a coven, a female witch, who has been initiated into the 3rd degree. Abbreviated as HPS in written rituals.

Higher Self - referred to as non-physical or one's true self. The enlightened, (actual) persona of the person, not to be confused with what the person thinks they are.

Hiving Off - The process where some members of a coven break off to form a new coven of their own.

Holy Grail - Thought of as a symbol of purity and love. It is believed that the chalice was used to hold the blood of Christ from the cross. To some, the Grail is a physical chalice. To others it represents the royal bloodline of Christ and the womb.

Horned God - The lord of the animals and of the forests. He is associated with hunting. Often mistaken and associated with Satan (an incorrect assumption). He is a consort of the Goddess.

Hydromancy - Divination by liquid, especially water.

I

Imbas - A source of inspiration, a fire in the head. The source of magick and divine inspiration.

Imbolc - The February 2nd festival the celebrates the first stirrings of Spring. The word is Gaelic in Nature and meaning "in the belly" as reference to the womb of Mother Nature.

Incantation; Incant - The spoken part of a spell.

Incense - The ritual burning of herbs, oils, or other aromatic items to scent the air during magick and ritual, and to better help the witch attune to the goal of the working. These include incense cones, incense sticks, and smudge sticks all of which are directly lit with an open flame as from a match or lighter, as well as powdered incense, which is burned over a hot charcoal rather than being directly lit itself.

The use of incense is very ancient, and in its earliest form it was probably thrown directly on the fire, or used to fuel the fire. Incense is used to raise the vibration of a place and to lend its own qualities to the energies being raised there. Some of the many different types of incense, which are commonly used include: Sage (cleansing and purification), Cinnamon (protection and prosperity), Rose (love), and Sandalwood (psychic opening).

Initiate - A person who has undertaken the rite of entry into a coven, circle, or other organization.

Initiation - Admission ceremony for an initiate to gain entry into a coven or circle. Generally, with the ritual of an oath of secrecy.

Intent - We do magic by consciously focusing energy. We shape that energy through thought and emotion. The energy takes its direction from the "intent" we set into that thought and emotion.

"Intent" is your goal or purpose, what you wish to achieve. And it is very important to be clear in intent. When you concentrate upon your intent during a magical working, you are imprinting the energy with your intent, so that it will shape itself to bring your intent to pass.

Invocation - Using chant or prayer to bring divine power into magick from the exterior into ritual. An Invocation is the acknowledgement of the deity and that they are present during the working.

Invoking - Summoning of an entity of a higher nature than human See Evoking.

Involution - The process of slowing the vibration of energy and increasing its intensity to make it more physical in nature. To Involve is to focus solely on a part of creation, assuming a spiritual tunnel vision. It is a way of blocking the rest of creation and separation from the Goddess affording a singularity in perception.

Inward Silence - The silencing of the emotions and thoughts that distract from the effectiveness of a ritual.

J &K

Jew-itch - A name created by Pagans who are Jewish in origin. These are people who are seeking out the pagan roots of their birth religion.

Julian Calendar - In 1582 Pope Gregory X111 introduced his Gregorian calendar, wiping out ten days to make it astronomically correct. Another day was later dropped. This new calendar replaced the older Julian one.

Kabala - Mystical teaching from the Jewish-Gnostic tradition. These traditions include Ceremonial Magick and the Alexandrian and are based in these teachings. Also, Qabala.

Karma - Originating in Hindu philosophy, it is the method used to explain injustice and reprisal. The idea is that in this life if you wrong another, they will be avenged in the next life. So basically, "What goes around, comes around". Any actions you issue either good or bad will be returned onto you. In Karma, you must learn the responsibility of your actions. You have to learn the lesson or the event can happen over and over again until the lesson is learned.

Keys - In simple terms, something that can help you shift consciousness. It can be anything that helps evoke the right atmosphere and mental state to make the shift easier to accomplish. They make it easier to shift into our higher selves.

An example of a key is candlelight. A candle has a flame which can be focused upon. Similar items can be crystal or something that represents a focal point. The thing is to use the key to help shift consciousness, and connect with Higher Self.

Ki - Japanese word for the universal life force, synonymous with the Chinese term, Chi.

Kitchen Magick; Kitchen Witchcraft - A more easily attained way to practice witchcraft in your home on a budget. Usually practiced in suburban or lower budget situations. It allows witches to utilize household items instead of the often difficult to obtain ritual items

L

Labrys - A double-headed ax symbolizes the Goddess in her Lunar phase. It has roots in ancient Crete.

Labyrinth - A representation of the soul's journey through life from birth to death. It is a maze of tunnels and passageways that lead from an outer point to a center through a particular design.

Lamen - Worn during rituals, it is a round disc made of metal with magickal symbols on it.

Lammas - A pagan Sabbat which takes place on August 1st.

Law Of Three - A concept similar to Karma. It is a learning experience. Most Wiccans believe that if you do good or bad by someone it will come back to you three-fold. Some take this literally, others believe that when the lesson is learned, then Karma is satisfied.

Left-hand Path - A less than positive term. Meaning people who feel justified in using magick for purposes less than constructive and forced on other human beings.

Levitation - A supernatural experience, where a body is suspended in mid air without the help of any physical support.

Libation - In ritual, it is the act of offering a portion of your food and drink to a deity, nature spirit or ancestor. In many spells, it is symbolized by pouring a bit of liquid on the Earth.

Litha - The Summer Solstice festival, celebrated on or about June 21.

Lithomancy - Divination by stones.

Loa - An ancestral deity in the Vodou religion.

Lower Self - The parts of our existence that we are aware of in everyday life. These being: the physical, the emotional, and the mental aspects of our being.

Through the act of meditation, we can access out Higher Selves. This act includes astral and creative levels of our beings, as well as, those traits that aspects that make us a distinct aspect of Deity (the level on which we are Divine but separate). It is also where we seek the Devine level where we strive to be all as one.

Lughnasadh, Lunasa (Festival of Lugh) - The Autumn festival celebrated on July 31. Gaelic in origin, the name of the month of August, and is pronounced "LOO-na-sa".

Lycanthropy - the ability of a person or witch to change into an animal. Often used to refer to people who change into werewolves.

M

Mabon - The Fall Equinox festival, celebrated on or about September 22.

Macrocosm - In reference to the Microcosm, it is the Cosmos as a whole. In human terms, it's manifestation.

Mage - A master in the art of Magick. Focused on mind, body and spirit, they prefer not to use tools to perform magick. To be a mage, you have to be scholarly and skilled at a high level.

Magick - In basic terms, magick is a process of using your personal will and emotional power to bring about changes in yourself and the world around you. The use of magick is neither good or evil, positive or negative. It is your "will" that determines the outcome and the path it will take.

Magick is not connected to spirituality. Magick can be practiced and a person still be spiritual in nature. Most people either choose one path or the other. Both Meditation and prayer can be seen as ways to practice magick. Magick is brought to life through the focus of will power and emotion, which form and shape energy. Magick should mostly be used for self-improvement, prosperity, protection and healing.

Magick Circle - A sphere constructed of personal power. A place where rituals are usually performed. A place of protection where witches can enact ceremonial magick. The sphere not only surrounds in a circle but goes above and below ground to protect at all angles.

Magickal Name - A name chosen by the dedicant or initiate to symbolize rebirth into their new path.

Magickal System - The basic set of guidelines relating to the worship of specific Gods and Goddesses or cultural traditions.

Magickal Tools - Any item used by a witch or wiccan to bring about magick. These tools are often highly personal and have an attachment to the practitioner. A wiccan's magickal tools are usually; the Athame or magickal blade, the Wand, the Chalice, and the Pentacle. The same tools are the basis of the Tarot.

Magickal Voice, the - The projected powerful voice used to read aloud words during rituals. The voice should possess no doubt or insecurity. This is all inclusive in speaking, singing, and whispers.

Magus - A male occult adapt.

Maiden - **1.** Used to refer to one of the members of a coven, usually the assistant to the High Priestess. **2.** Also one of aspects of the triple goddess (maiden, mother, crone). She is symbolized by the waxing moon, creation, and the time between Beltane and Imbolc.

Male Mysteries - An area of study that tries to reclaim the power and mystery of the old Gods for modern Pagan males.

Matrifocal - A term used to refer to a time when family life centered around or lived near clan matriarch. Denotes pre-patriarchal.

May Pole - Representing the phallus a sexual symbol of Beltane.

Meditation - A process of focusing inward. Inverting the mind to pay attention to inner silence and avoiding outer chaos.

Some other forms of meditation focus on the outer chaos. This practice is encouraged mostly in Buddhism, but is accepted in almost all religions.

Megalith - A huge stone monument or structure. Stonehenge would be a prime example of this.

Menhir - A huge stone probably erected by early peoples for religious, spiritual, or magickal reasons.

Mentor - An elder magickal practitioner who offers advice and guidance.

Merry Meet - In simple terms, it means "Greetings". It is a greeting commonly used by Pagans and Wiccans. Abbreviated as MM.

Merry Part - In simple terms, it means "Good-bye". It is a greeting commonly used by Pagans and Wiccans. Abbreviated as MP.

Metaphysical - Having the nature of or being a part of metaphysics.

Metaphysics - The area of philosophy and abstract thought about topics which are not physical in nature. These areas include but are not limited to existence, the soul, supernatural, astral travel and others.

Microcosm - The Physical World. The Lesser world. It parallels the greater world or Macrocosm. The world within us all.

Midsummer - Sabbat celebrated in June.

Midwinter - Sabbat celebrated in June – Winter Solstice in the Southern Hemisphere. December 21 to 22 each year in the Northern Hemisphere.

Mojo - Magick.

Mojo Bag - A small bag filled with charms, herbs, and stones, generally worn around the neck which is charged with energies to perform a certain goal.

Monotheism - Belief in one supreme deity who has no other forms and displays no other aspects.

Mother - The Goddess representing motherhood, mid-life, and fertility. Her Sabbats are Midsummer and Lughnasadh. She is represented by the full moon phase, the egg, the colors red and green.

Muir - The sea.

Music Of The Spheres - Each of the seven spheres has an energy vibrations all its own. The vibrations are attuned to a certain sound. They are representational just as when a voice sings and a drum beats, they have their own vibration. As the energy of the spheres vibrates, it too must create a sound. This is the idea behind the "music of the spheres".

The idea of energy and vibrations is directly tied to the Chakra system. In this, vibrating sound is used in energy work involves the linking of seven-vowel sound with the seven planes/bodies/Chakras.

Myth - Cycles body of lore about any land or people that makes up their mythology.

N

Necromancy - **1.** A way of revealing the future through magick and communication with spirits. **2.** The act of summoning the souls of the dead.

Necronomicon - A pseudo-grimoire. Believed to be a source of occult information, it was written by an unknown author and mentioned in a book written by H. P. Lovecraft.

Neo-Pagan - In general terms, a new pagan. A branch from Paganism, it is a modern earth religion. It is based on ancient pre-Christian religious practices. Wicca, may be considered a neo-pagan religion, being it is derived from ancient witchcraft and paganism.

Neophyte - A trainee practitioner who is studying the ways of the old religion under guidance from an adept in the magickal craft. Neophyte designated the first level of training. In the second level of training a practitioner can be considered for the position of Priest or Priestess.

New Age - The modern movement which involves combining metaphysical concepts with the practice of an organized religion.

New Religion - Pagan term used in reference to Christianity.

Nursery Rhyme - A poem written for the amusement of children over the years much of Pagan lore was hidden in these rhymes. This was mostly in the years of witch persecutions.

O

Oath of Wicca - A binding oath to protect Wiccan secrets.

OBE - The shortened form of Out-of-body experience.

Occult - The study of and science of things esoteric, secret, paranormal, and supernatural.

Occultist - One who practices and or studies a variety of occult subjects.

Offering - A gift dedicated or offered to a Deity, or Spirit. This gift or offering is symbolic in nature, and is an act of respect to a certain Deity or God. It is meant to strengthen the bond between the one offering and the Spirit. It is not thought of as a way to give sustenance to the Deity or spirit. Often thought of as a votive offering for example, given in fulfillment of a vow.

Ogham - The magickal Celtic alphabet made up of 20 letters called Fews, each representing a different tree.

Old Ones - The A term which refers to all aspects of the Goddess and God.

Old Religion - A term used in Wicca and Witchcraft. It is used because Witchcraft is often thought to have descended from the old Pagan beliefs. It is however misleading when used in reference to Wicca which is a much newer religion based on the practices of Witchcraft.

Omen - A believed sign of good or evil. It can be small and yet significant, maybe as simple as a spilling of water or something breaking in your presence.

Omens - The plural form of Omen. A message from the spirit world delivered in symbolic terms. They are personal in nature and have meaning to the person receiving. Some examples of these symbols would be the appearance of a black cat or the black dog omen. It is believed that these omens are not by chance and could have happened for no other reason than to deliver a message.

Oneiromancy - Divination through dreams.

Ophion And Eurynome - Eurynome is a very ancient Greek Moon Goddess. Her name means "Far Wanderer". In myth Eurynome and Ophion are Goddess and God, from Whose union arises all creation.

Oracle - Similar to someone who can channel, it is a person who can be used as a conduit to communicate with spirits from the other side. An example would be an Oracle, who is given questions to ask spirits and who obtains insight form the other side.

Ostara - The Sabbat in which the arrival of Spring is celebrated. Christians created their celebration of Easter to coincide with this celebration. The celebration is in named for the goddess of Spring and is celebrated with eggs and rabbits as symbols.

Outer Court - Temples have both Inner and Outer Courts. The Inner court is made up the clergy residing in the Temple. The Outer court's members participate in ceremonies but are not required to attend or train for clergy.

P

Pagan - Originating from Latin Paganus the word means country dweller or villager. In modern terms it has been adapted to mean a follower of Wicca or a similar magick embracing community. Many believe the term should be Neo-pagan in reference to the belief that Wiccans being over time the ways of the culture have advanced and changed. Pagans are not Satanists.

Pagandom - Part of the world inhabited mainly by Pagans.

Paganing - The celebration when a baby or child is presented in a circle to the God or Goddess to be given a name to use in the craft. When the child reaches the age of 13, they can choose their own name as a part of their Coming of Age ceremony.

Paganism - Generally thought of as an Earth religion, it is any that is not based on Christian, Islam or Judaism beliefs. Most have more than one God or Goddess. The word means "country dweller".

Pagan Standard Time - A term slang in nature referring to people who cannot arrive on time for an event or get someplace on time. The term is outdated and no longer used. Abbreviated as PST.

Pallomancy - Divination with a pendulum.

Pantheism - A belief in many deities who are really the same. Each one is but a part of a single deity but representative of a feature. Paganism is pantheistic.

Pantheon - A grouping of Gods or Goddesses within a particular religion. Mostly separated by region it is for example the Greek Gods.

Passion Over Ritual - Ritual observed when a loved one has died.

Past Life Regression - The process to recall a previous live. It is often attained when a person is put in a deep hypnotic trance and transgressed back to their past life when their soul was in another body. The process requires a belief that the soul exists. The concept is a sound one being, that if a soul exists, then the mind has stored memories from all past lives and they should be able to be accessed by regression to that life.

Path Working - Often called Vision Questing, it is the process of using astral projection, bi-location, or dream time to accomplish a specific goal.

Pathfinder - Spritual guide, help, or tool.

Patriarchal - A term to refer to a more modern society where the male deities are worshiped. It replaced the time of matriarchal clans which worshiped goddesses.

Patron Deity - The God or Goddess one feels the most comfortable worshiping. Most people observe more than one deity but there is always one that appeals over the others. Any Deity that you are drawn to can be your Patron Deity. One's Patron Deity is the one you seek guidance, visions, and blessing, from.

Pecti-Wita - A Scottish tradition of Wicca. See also Wita.

Pendulum - A tool used to communicate with the Devine for contacting spirits. Usually a string with items, such as a crystal or ring or such attached at the bottom. It can be used for divination purposes. One end is held in the hand while the other is allowed to swing freely. The movement of the pendulum is said to offer an answer to questions asked. It is a tool which contacts the psychic mind.

Pentacle - It is a circle whose outer edge encompasses the five points of the pentagram. It is also work in adornment as a symbol of a witch's belief system and to celebrate magickal work and ceremonies. Each point on the star is in reference to the elements: Earth, Air, Fire, Water, and Spirit. The inverted pentagram is used in some second-degree initiations, to indicate a function of growth.

Pentagram - A five-pointed star often associated with witchcraft, Paganism and occultism. In the United States it is always displayed with the single point upwards due to some groups using the two points upward to symbolize Satanism.

In Great Britain, having two-points-upwards is the symbol of the Wiccan Second Degree. Many British Wiccans are abandoning the two-points-upward symbol as relations with American Pagans increases. The pentagram is a symbol of protection and is not evil.

Pentalpha - Referred to as "Five A's" was the sacred symbol of the Pythagoreans. Today it is more familiarly known as the Pentagram. The Pythagoreans used the pentalpha and the five Tetraktys triangles to convey many metaphysical beliefs.

Personal Deity - Any one of the faces of the Universal Deity that we choose to relate to. Personal Deities are individual aspects of the Universal Deity portrayed in very human terms. Personal Deities are there to guide us in our understanding of the Deity, and make a personal and emotional, connection.

Personal Power - The energy that sustains us. It is given to us by the God or Goddess. We receive it at conception, while still in the womb and later in life from food and drink. It is also given to us through such items as the Sun and the Moon.

Philtre - A potion, especially for love.

Phrenology - Character analysis by studying the shape and surface of the skull.

Polarity - The concept that there are two equal but separate energies. They are balanced between positive and negative. An example is the Yin and the Yang. The bring about universal balance. Other ideas of Polarity include: birth/death, dark/light, God/Goddess.

Polytheism - A belief that there are many unrelated deities, and that they all have their own domain and interests. They are believed to have no spiritual or familial relation to each other.

Poppets - Anthropomorphic dolls used when casting spells as a likeness for a human being.

Projective Hand - Used in ritualism, a term to describe your most powerful hand. It is generally the one you write with.

Prana - Permeating through everything, it is the vital force of the Cosmos as it operates on the Etheric level.

Priest - A male who is dedicated to his deities and human kind. A High Priest is the leader of a Coven or Wiccan organization. He can play the role of god in some ceremonial situations.

Priestess - A female who is dedicated to her deities and human kind. A High Priestess is the leader of a Coven or Wiccan organization. She can play the role of goddess in some ceremonial situations. A Solitary Witch can be become a priestess by dedicating herself to a particular God or Goddess.

Precession Of The Equinoxes - "Motion of the points where the Sun crosses the celestial equator, caused by precession of Earth's axis. Hipparchus noticed that the stars' positions were shifted consistently from earlier measures, indicating that Earth, not the stars, was moving. This precession, a wobbling in the orientation of Earth's axis with a cycle of almost 26,000 years, is caused by the gravity of the Sun and the Moon acting on Earth's equatorial bulge. The planets also have a small influence on precession. Projecting Earth's axis onto the celestial sphere locates the northern and southern celestial poles. Precession makes these points trace out circles on the sky and also makes the celestial equator wobble, changing its points of intersection (equinoxes) with the ecliptic."

Priest - This is a male that is devoted to the service of his chosen deity and humankind.

Priestess - Is a female that is devoted to the service of her chosen deity and humankind.

Primeval Deity - Being both feminine and masculine, both spiritual and physical, it is the God/Goddess before creation. Primeval Deity is both the beginning and the end of existence. It is the inner soul of all creation. It is often represented as the Androgyne or the Crone.

Projective Hand - A term often used in ritualism to describe your right hand, the sending hand.

Prophet - One who receives inspiration, information, or insights into the future from a divine source.

Psi - (Pronounced "sie") Anything relating to psychic, magick, or other supernatural abilities.

Psionics - The use of psychic powers to affect or manipulate the physical world.

Psionicist - One who uses psionics.

Psychic Abilities - The receiving or transferring of information about the five senses. (sight, touch, hearing, taste, smell).

Psychic Awareness - A state of awareness where the conscious mind can tap into the psychic mind.

Psychic Mind - The Subconscious or Unconscious mind. It is where we are psychically aware. It is a place where we can receive psychic messages. It comes alive when we sleep and often exists when we dream and meditate. It is our direct link with the Divine, and nonphysical world around us.

Psychic Shielding - Strengthening of one's aura to keep out inappropriate or unwanted energies.

Psychic Tide - The eternal cycles of energy in the Universe. They move in a constant process of Involution and Evolution. Everything that exists moves in the rhythm of the Psychic Tide.

Psychism - Psychism is the art of using powers of the soul passively, to receive information or communication from the Higher Self. Magick and Psychism are connected, and the only division between them is there to make understanding easier.

Psychometry - Holding or touching an object and receiving images, impressions, or vibes from it.

Pyromancy - Divination by fire.

Q

Qabala - Jewish mysticism; metaphysical practices based on the Judaic Qabalistic texts.

Quarter Days - The old Celtic festivals of Samhain, Bride, Beltaine, and Lughnassadh. The solstices and equinoxes. These days carry power with them to heighten the use of power for charms, spells, and divination. Bonfires are lit for the protection and cleansing of the people and animals, and recognition of Gods and Goddess are preformed. These days are often thought to be lucky.

Quarters - The North, East, South, and West parts of a circle, often represent the four watchtowers.

R

Receptive Hand - The hand with lesser power. You have one dominant and one receptive. It is generally the one you do not write with. "This hand is used less in holding and charging ritual items, however, it receives outside energy which is used to feed the magick."

Rede - A tenet, rule, doctrine, or law.

Reincarnation - Simply put, a rebirth from one life to the next. It is the return of the soul to physical form. The new physical form can be animal or human.

Reiving - Clearing a space, to psychically clear unwanted entities both positive and negative.

Releasing - To allow the extra energy you have to be released. In this process the power can be grounded and returned to Mother Earth to be used in more productive ways.

Right-hand Path - Opposite of left-hand path, it is a term used to refer to a person who practices magick for the benefit of others.

Rite - A ritual.

Ritual - A ceremony (mental/physical) to perform specific magick or to pay tribute to a Deity or chosen pantheon.

Ritual Ceremony - In Wicca it is a religious ceremony meant to heighten a connection with the divine. It can also be an act that is performed to produce a desired effect, I.E. Object manipulation. Through magick, the process allows a practitioner to enter a state where it is easier to apply energy to a desired task.

Ritual Consciousness - An altered state of awareness that is needed for the successful manipulation of the environment to perform magick. Often achieved through ritual and visualization, it is a state where the physical and psychic mind are in tune. In this state magick senses the energies and directs them towards a purpose and guides them to a specific goal. It is a linking of nature with Deity to expand awareness.

Ritual Tools - A general term for tools used to perform magick. Used by Wiccans and Witches, these tools usually represent an element.

Rune - An object used in magick and for divination purposes. There are many different types of Runes including Anglo-Saxon, Norse, and modern Wiccan runes. Each of these Runes represents an alphabet of some sort. They can be tossed or mixed up in a bag and then drawn once a question is decided to give an answer. These Runes are deciphered based on location tossed or by a Rune layout.

Runestones - Divination through the use of Teutonic figures or pictographs where certain meanings are applied. Runes originated from the Norse people's alphabet. Runes can be used for magick or divination purposes. Instead of the random usage for divination, Runestones can be placed in a certain order to create a future.

S

Sabbat - In Wicca there are eight solar festivals. These include four solstices and equinoxes, and four dates between them. These festivals include Yule, Imbolc, Ostara, Beltane, Litha, Lughnasadh, Mabon, and Samhain.

Sadhus - In Hindu and Jain religion the term means a "holy person". Their main purpose in life is to achieve inner peace through meditation and spirituality. To better connect with the inner essence, they wear little or no clothing. One holy person who attained worldwide recognition and wore just a loincloth was Mahatma Gandhi. Jain religion was founded by Mahavira, a group of holy people who choose to go completely named. It was from these people the term "skyclad" was created.

Salamander - The traditional term for a Fire Elemental.

Samhain - The Sabbat ritual celebrated at the end of October in the Northern Hemisphere, known by many as Hollowe'en. The name in Gaelic for the month of November, it is pronounced SOW'en.

Sands of Time - In reference to the Sphinx or Egypt, it is sand taken from between its paws.

Satanism - To believe in Satanism, it is necessary to recognize the Christian religion. It is a backwards form of Christianity where the Devil or Satan is revered as a god and the Lord's Prayer is recited backwards to perform their version or a Black Mass.

One famous Satanist Group was the Hellfire Club of which notable figures like Benjamin Franklin and Aleister Crowley were members. It is important to note that Satanism has nothing to do with Wicca or Witchcraft. In order to believe in Satan you would have to believe in Christian beliefs. Wicca is an ancient, pre-Christian religion based on the ideas of fertility, nature, love and balance. Perhaps a confusion arises when some Satanists like to refer to themselves as Witches. Wiccans have a Rede that says, "An' it harm none, do what ye will" which prohibits harming anything else where Satanists have been reported to perform rituals that kill or maim animals or people.

Scarab - A symbol from ancient Egypt. It represents the continuation of life through the process of rebirth. The Scarab was considered a sacred insect.

Scourge - A symbol of mercy, it is a ritual whip symbolizing firmness. Most are made of silk and harmless. They are more for ceremonial purposes than to bring harm.

Scrying - A form of divination the involved starring into or gazing upon an object or thing. Items used can be but are not limited to: a crystal ball, water, a black mirror, and glass. It is believed that the scryer can see vision in these objects of things that are yet to come. They can also gain knowledge of past events and present ones through the five senses.

Seven Great Powers - These include the seven basic archetypes perceived from the Personal Deities. Matched to the seven planets of Ptolemaic astrology, they are: Goddess -Maiden, Mother, crone. God -Young God, Hero (Sun) God, King, Sorcerer.

Shade - The spirit of a being which refuses to leave the physical plane.

Shaman - A person male or female, who gains knowledge and experience through an altered state of consciousness. There are many types of ritual that allow the Shaman to pierce the veil of the physical world and the realm of energies. The knowledge acquired is meant to assist in changing his or her world for the better through magick.

Shamanism - The religion practiced by the ancients of several locations which allows a Shamans to communicate with the spirit world. Often associated with Native Americans, the power they posses allows for animism, possession, prophecy/revelations, shape shifting, and soul travel.

Shape shifting - A practice that involves the changing or morphing of human form. While it is rumored this can be accomplished on the physical plane, it is often referred to as happening on the Astral plane. This practice is not shared publicly and very few books are available about it. It is said the practice is kept in secret and only handed down through teacher to student.

Shields - A protective barrier of power erected around a person, place, or object.

Shifting Consciousness - Rising above our normal consciousness to connect with our Higher Self. It is in the higher level of consciousness that magick is practiced. During this process, the state of normal brain waves is altered and there is a shift in consciousness that is measureable.

Shillelagh - Usually made from blackthorn wood, it is a magickal tool corresponding to the staff in other traditions.

Showstone - A crystal ball or sphere used for divination, especially scrying.

Sidhe - pronounced (shee). In reference to faeries or other world beings.

Sigil - A form of magick seal to close something. This can be a sign, or glyph. These are most powerful when you create them yourself using your own intent and power. These can be used to seal documents, letters, or packages.

Silence - There are two types of Silence:
-Active silence: Is referred to when a practitioner uses background noise as an aid. (i.e.: music, the sound of the ocean, thunderstorms, the wind in the trees,).

-Passive silence: Is referred to when there is no sound and complete silence.

Simple Feast - A ritual meal shared with the Goddess and God.

Sky Father - Shamanistic in origin. It assigns deification to the sky as a male entity.

Skyclad - The act of performing magick or magickal acts in the nude. The religion of Mahavira coined the term "skyclad" as they often were completely nude and found no need for clothing. The practice was not typical in the old days for fear of clothing being stolen (they usually had few clothes), or if discovered doing witchcraft in the nude, it would hinder their escape.

Smudging - Ritual cleansing that involved the use of burning herbs to remove negative energy or spirits from a location. Native Americans achieved this by burning sage sticks and chanting while waving a feather to spread the smoke into all corners of a home or dwelling.

Solar Circuit - As in reference to the Solar Chakra, it is the principle energy circuit of the human body. It is at this point that energy enters the body from its higher self. It is said the practice of tapping into this limited energy source may be restricted or blocked. The Solar Circuit is manly for sustenance of the body and prolonging physical life.

Solitary - A witch who practices alone instead of within a coven.

Solo Witch - a solo witch is one who that practices witchcraft alone.

So Mote it Be - A phrase that literally means, "So it shall be". It is used often in rituals to close a chant or incantation.

Sorcery - A practice, magickal in nature, that is used to summon, bind or banish a deity. Sorcerers usually do not use tools to practice magick.

Soul - The immortal self, a human being's true identity. the part of us that surpasses death. This part is believed to be reincarnated after a time in the otherworld.

Spell - The use of mental and emotional energy to bring about a change in the physical world need to accomplish a goal. This process focuses energy through, words that are spoken aloud, drawn or even acted out through bodily movements. To work, you have to be focused and have clear intent and need and supply energy to create the desired effect.

Spell-crafting - The practice of creating spells by writing ideas, arranging corresponding items and creating incantations.

Spiral - A symbol of "coming into being", a sacred spiral is an important part of magickal workings.

Spirit Guides - A guide who helps us in everyday life. One who helps us when dealing with life lessons. Every person has a number of Spirit Guides, or Familiars, around them. They are also act as advisors to those who are willing to listen.

Spirit guides may be a representation of people we have known. Someone we still have a connection with. These people may be ones we have known in this lifetime. In other cases, they be someone from a past life which is still associated with us. We may have no conscious memory of the person.

A person can have more than one spirit guide, but usually they will associate with one main guide. This spirit is destined to be a companion through life. There are many different types of guides, some specialize in developing a certain area or talent while some are meant to heal. They may be guiding or helping you and you may not be aware of it.

In Ancient Times Spirit Guides were referred to as Fairies. This was before the term was attached to nature. Some may call them Guardian Angels. No matter what the name the help offered is the same in the journey through life.

Spirits - Entities which are free of a physical body.

Staff - Ritual tool which corresponds to the wand or athame.

Stang - A term from Pagan Rome, meaning a ritual tool which resembles a two-pronged trident. This object is often used as a replacement in magick for a wand or circle.

Subconscious Mind - A part of our consciousness that is not readily available to us. A part of the mind which functions in the background during the course of a normal day. It is the area where dreams are stored and symbolic knowledge is waiting to be available. It contains the most minute details of every experience.

Summerland - The Pagan Land of the Dead.

Summoner - The male version of the maiden, a member of a coven and a person who is an assistant to the High Priest.

Sylph - The traditional term for an Air Elemental.

Symbol - A sign or concept that represents something else. In some cases, symbols are used to represent gods, elements and goals. Objects can be symbols, such as a chalice representing life from the god or goddess.

Sympathetic Magick - A form of magick where like things attract. It is based on the idea of sympathy. It means like items which have similar meanings can be used to represent each other.

For example, if plants are green and plants grow, then green can represent the color for growth. If you were practicing candle magick and you were casting a spell for growth or prosperity, you would burn a green candle.

Since fire can bring about a change or transformation, it can be used to cast spells. Burning a paper with a spell or charm can transform and power your spell.

These processes are basically "keys". See "Keys" in the dictionary list. They are symbolic tools that we use to focus our energy. From this we use our intent to bring about the desired change.

Synchronicity - A Jungian term meaning a coincidence which seems to have meaning is not yet clear.

T

Talisman - An object that has been magickally charged in order to bring a change or to bring something to the wearer.

Tarot - Cards used in Divination. They usually consist of a deck of 78. The cards connect the practitioner with energy that can be used to determine a wide range of information and used to help decide answers. They can also be used as a part of specific rituals.

Tarot Cards - (pronounced: Ta-RO) A system of divination similar to the casting of Runes (See Runes). The symbols printed on these cards all have depictions of situations and states of being. The structure of Tarot is much more complex than that of Runes and when cards are spread, there are many different layouts and opportunities for information to be gathered.

Tarologist - One adept at the art and science of handling the Tarot.

Tasseography - Divination by the reading of tea leaves.

Telekinesis - A form of psycho kinesis which involves moving objects with the mind. Items moved are in no way touched by physical means.

Telepathy - Psychic communication between two minds without the need of speaking aloud.

The Deepening - The Second and Third Degree Rites.

Thelema - Religious beliefs that are founded on magic within the Christian pantheon.

Theurgy - Magick involving the use of divine spirits and oneness or closeness with one's God or Deities.

Third Eye - Located in the middle of the forehead, it is the psychic eye, not physically visible.

Three-fold Law - A Wiccan principle which originated from the teachings of Gerald Gardner. A concept similar to Karma. It is a learning experience. Most Wiccans believe that if you do good or bad by someone it will come back to you three-fold. Some take this literally, others believe that when the lesson is learned, then Karma is satisfied.

Thurible - An incense burner suspended on a chain. It can be hung or swung to spread the smoke through a room or given area.

Normally used with powdered incense and charcoal, Thurible is very ancient, and historical examples exist.

Tir-nan-og - Meaning "Land of the Young," or "Faerie Land", it is believed by Celts that upon death, the soul enters this place.

Torc - "In Celtic religion the Torc, a circular metal necklace, was a symbol of initiation and of the Divine Mysteries. The Torc's circular shape reflects the cyclical nature of reality and the ancient concept of Ourobouros, representing the idea that all things ultimately return to their source. Sacred to Cernunnos-Secculos-Dagda, the Celtic Lord of the Dead and of the Spirit realms, the Torc was not only worn as a symbol of initiation, but was also used as a symbol of all things magical and spiritual, and was frequently hung up in a house to confer protection -in which use it was later replaced by the horse shoe."

Totem - An animal which teaches a lesson through symbolism. Totem energy can be used to practice magick and Pagans may wear the symbols of these animals. these symbols carry specific messages, like a bear for strength or a rabbit for agility.

Totem Animal - Derived from Native American spirituality, it is a spirit guide in the form of an animal who chooses to accompany you.

Tradition - 1. Branch of paganism followed by any individual Pagan or coven. **2.** Type of teachings etc used by a High Priest or Priestess of a coven. By using their surname they introduce a particular spirituality followed by a practitioner.

This is a relatively new concept invented by Gardner and is mixed up with a particular pathway of witchcraft such as: Green Witchcraft, Fairy Wicca, Air Witch and others. Not to be confused with a pantheon: Egyptian (Fellowship of Isis), Norse (Asatru), Greek, Celtic, Strega.

Traditional - Groups which practice Wicca. Each tradition has a different set of rules and guidelines by which it follows. Examples of traditions are Gardnerian, Alexandrian, Celtic, Faery, and Strega.

Tradition, Wicca - An organized, structured, Wiccan subgroup. Some Wiccans follow no specific tradition which would be eclectic Wicca. Common examples of Tradition include Garnerian, Seax, Dianic, Faery, Pecti, Teutonic, Caledoni, Alexandrian, and many others...

Traditions - Sects or groups which practice Wicca. Each tradition has a different set of rules and guidelines by which it follows.

Transmutation - The work of alchemy, changing base metals and elements into precious things.

Tree Calendar - With 13 lunar months of the year, it is the Celtic system of reckoning by assigning each a sacred tree.

Trilithon - A stone arch made from two upright slabs with one lying atop these. They are featured in Stonehenge.

Triple Goddess - the principle female deity of witch craft.

Tuatha De Dannan - Meaning "Children of the Goddess Dana," or the ancient Faerie Gods and Goddesses.

Tuathail - A term that means moving in a direction opposite that of the Sun around the Earth. It is used to indicate clockwise movement (Southern Hemisphere) counter-clockwise movement (Northern Hemisphere). From Gaelic Tuath it literally means Northward. For example, Tuathail movement is used when the Magick Circle is being taken down.

U

Ululation - The part of an incantation or chant which demands full vocal force and volume.

Uncasting - Opening the circle at the end of a ritual.

Undine - The traditional term for a Water Elemental.

Universal Deity - All the faces of the Deity and the ways these faces are understood. That infinite power is Universal Deity -the spirit of Deity that is beyond all names and images.

Unmanifest - The unknown source of existence, it is said that magicians take their power from the un-manifest to use it within the manifest.

V

Vampirism - The practice drawing energy from the life force of another. Commonly this is blood, other times it is life force taken psychically.

Vangello Delle Streghe - Published by Charles Leland in 1599, Under with the title "Aradia, or the Gospel of the Witches", it is book containing Wiccan Scripture, the story of creation, a collection of myths from Italian Witchcraft, and the Charge Of The Goddess.

Veil - The separation between what we consciously recognize being ourselves, and our higher power is called a veil. Most people are not even aware of the veil, with the exception of those who are "Born Old". See Born Old. The mental self, its thoughts, and the higher aspects of the being, from which we derive such abilities as clairvoyance, telepathy, telekinesis, are the veil.

Veil of Unknowing - The boundary between the manifest and the un-manifest.

Vibration - It is the rate that energy moves down the seven spheres. The further it goes the weaker it gets. The weaker it gets, the slower it will become. When it is at its slowest, it is more attuned to the physical plane. When energy moves upward from a lower level, it generates heat. The opposite is also true, when energy moves downward it produces coldness.

Virgin - Also known as the Maiden, she is the youngest aspect of the Triple Goddess. She is represented by the waxing moon; the Sabbats are Imbolc and Ostara and her colors white and blue.

Virtues - The properties, of magick granted to plants, stones, creatures and herbs during divine creation.

Vision Quest - Also called path working, it is the use of astral projection, bi-location, or dream time to accomplish a specific task.

Vision Questing - Also called path working. See Vision Quest.

Visualization - **1**. Used in magick to focus and direct ones energy, towards a goal. **2**. Creating a mental image of a person, place or happening with clear intent. This is often accomplished through meditation and allows a practitioner to enter a private place where magick can be created and executed.

Voodoo - Derived form Catholicism and African god worship, it is a Polytheistic religion.

Vortices - Just as in the body there are Chakra energy centers, the same is true of the Earth. The areas are called Vortices. In these areas, the Earth's energy is higher and power from these areas can be used to charge spells and magick. Vortices are usually considered sacred spots, and are often used as worship centers. As in Chakras, the body's centers are connected by meridians where energy is transmitted, so the Earth has "Ley Lines" which connect its Vortices.

W

Wand - A ritual tool often used in Wicca, it's main purpose is to direct the flow of energy to a specific purpose. Wiccan's usually choose between wand and athame for magick purposes, however, the athame is the clear choice for casting circles. Most Wiccans choose the wand when summoning a God or Goddess.

Waning - In the lunar phase, it is when the moon is getting smaller and more in the shape of crescent. Traditionally this is when spells are cast that involve banishing, changing habits and eliminating things are performed. It is the opposite of waxing. See Waxing Moon.

Ward - A protection spell.

Warlock - A negative term in Wicca, it is often incorrectly used to refer to a male witch. The term if a male or female is simply witch. The term means "oath breaker". Most Witches find the term offensive.

Watchtowers - In modern Wicca and magick, there are four watchtowers that represent a cardinal direction, element, elemental, and a color. These are mainly used in ceremonial magick.

Waxing - The phase of the moon where it is getting larger. Nearly a full moon but not quite all the way there. This is the time to cast spells for growth and ones that bring things to you. The opposite of a waning moon. See Waning Moon.

Web weaving - Networking with other Pagans for friendship and the sharing of ideas and concepts.

Wheel of the Year - One full cycle of the seasons, in pagan beliefs in begins on the Sabbat of Samhain at the end of October.

White Handled Knife - Often referred to as The Athame and the White Handled Knife it is sometimes called the Boleen or Burrin. The use of the is purely symbolic and most Wiccans have two of these knives for different purposes. The White handle knife is generally used for all candle engraving and cutting purposes.

White Magick - A positive form of magick performed only in harmless acts. It is the form of magick that is practiced by most witches who do not recognize white or dark magick.

Wicca - A neo-pagan religion which has its roots in nature as a manifestation of the Devine. With a polytheistic view, Wiccans view Deity as a God or Goddess. Wiccan embraces magick and reincarnation. The belief system is in no way connected to Satanism.

Wiccan - 1. A person who follows or practices Wicca. **2**. Anything related to Wicca. (Examples include a Book Of Shadows, Good or Goddess)

Wiccaning - The Wiccan equivalent of a Christening.

Wiccan Rede - The law of Wicca which states that all may do as they wish, as long as they harm no living thing.

Wiccan Trilogy - The triple aspect of the goddess: Maiden, Mother, and Crone.

Wicce - Synonymous with Wicca. In some customs, Wicce is used for women and Wicca is used for men.

Widdershins - Direction of motion for banishing magic, counter-clockwise in the northern hemisphere, clockwise in southern.

Wild Ride - In Germanic mythology, the spirits of the dead were believed to ride out leading a great procession on certain nights, often during a full moon. The ride has been characterized as a "hunt." It was believed that the living could join this "ride" through the use of astral projection.

Wise Woman - A solitary female practitioner of witchcraft who gave charms and healing salves to villagers in Europe.

Wita - Scottish Wicca. See also Pecti-Wita.

Witch - A practitioner of witchcraft. There are many types and traditions of witches. A witch is not necessarily a Wiccan, though if a Wiccan practices witchcraft they can be called a witch.

Witch Ball - An 18th century tradition; a glass sphere hung in windows to ward off evil spirits. This is where the Christian concept of the Christmas tree ornament came from.

Witch Hazel - A potion that was used in divining and with dowsing rods to locate water or find hydration.

Witchcraft - The practice of spells and magick, often involving the worship of many deities or a supreme God or Goddess.

Witta - Irish Wicca.

Wizard - A name rarely used for Wiccans for male ceremonial magicians.

Word of Power - A word or name almost impossible to pronounce which is supposed to have great power when spoken. Most have no meaning in any language.

Working; Magickal Working - Any act involving magick or ritualism.

Wort - An archaic word for herb.

X, Y & Z

Yggdrasil - The Norse tree which provided the complex network of the universe. It held up the world and the heavens; its roots led to the underworld.

Younger Self - "Younger Self" is a term that is used to describe the part of the self, which is creative, spontaneous, and non-judgmental. Often thought of as a child and being the place of innocence. As a result of trauma, some people have cut themselves off from this place.

Yule - The Winter Solstice festival, December 22.

Yule Log - The traditional log burned at Yule ceremonies which most likely came from a pagan tradition for Yule celebration.

Zodiacal Age - A Zodiacal Age is a period used to mark time by a Zodiacal ruler and reflected in the Precession of the Equinoxes. Each Zodiacal Age is ruled by a sign of the Zodiac, from which the Age is said to take its character. We are currently at the Aquarian Age.

Zodiac - The Zodiac is a system of constellations used to structure the practice of Astrology. Astrology uses the theoretical position of stars and planets to address issues of internal character and future events.

Divination Dictionary

Aeromancy - A form of divination relating to the stars and astrology. A divination from the air, sky, and concentrating on cloud shapes, and other phenomena not normally visible in the heavens.

Alchemy - The practice of transforming of base metals into precious ones like gold or silver.

Alectryomancy - A form of divination where a bird picks grains from a circle that are associated with letters.

Aleuromancy - Divination similar to "fortune cookies", where answers to questions are rolled into balls of dough and once baked are chosen at random.

Alomancy - Divination by using table salt.

Alphitomancy - The use of a cake where it is digestible by a person with a clear conscience but is unpleasant to one who does not.

Anthropomancy - Divination by human sacrifice. This is against Wiccan beliefs and is outlawed.

Apantomancy - Divination through chance meetings with animals or other creatures. For example, when a black cat crosses your path.

Arithmancy or **Arithmomancy** - An early form of numerology where divination is made through numbers and the number value of letters.

Astraglomancy or **Astragyromancy** - Divination by dice where the faces of the dice bear numbers and letters.

Astrology - Divination using celestial bodies: the sun, moon, planets, and stars.

Augury - Divination by interpretations of signs and omens.

Austromancy - Divination by the study of the winds.

Axiomancy - Divination through how an axe or hatchet quivers or points when driven into post.

Belomancy - Divination performed by tossing or balancing arrows.

Bibliomancy - Divination by books.

Botanomancy - Divination from burning tree branches and leaves.

Capnomancy - Divination from the study of smoke rising from a fire.

Cartomancy - Divination by fortune telling using cards such as the Tarot.

Catoptromancy - Divination in the form of crystal gazing that utilizes a mirror turned to the moon to catch moonbeams.

Causimomancy - Divination based on the behavior of objects placed in a fire.

Cephalomancy - Divination with the skull or head of a donkey or goat.

Ceraunoscopy - Divination that seeks to draw omens from the study of thunder and lightning.

Ceroscopy - Divination in a form of fortune telling in which melted wax is poured into cold water.

Chiromancy - Divination from the lines on people's hands.

Chirognomy - Divination in the study of the general hand formation.

Clairaudience - Extra-sensory perception or "clear hearing" of divinatory information.

Clairvoyance - Extra-sensory perception or "clear seeing" of divinatory information.

Cleromancy - Divination by "casting lots", similar to dice but with objects such as pebbles or sea shells.

Clidomancy or **Cleidomancy** - Divination using a dangling key.

Coscinomancy - Divination using a hanging sieve

Critomancy - Divination by the study of barley cakes.

Cromniomancy - Divination using onion sprouts.

Crystallomancy - Divination through crystal gazing.

Cyclomancy - Divination in the form of a turning wheel.

Dactylomancy - Divination in an early form of Radiesthesia using a dangling ring.

Daphnomancy - Divination that requires one to listen to laurel branches crackling in an open fire.

Demonomancy - Divination with the aid of demons.

Dendromancy - Divination with either oak or mistletoe.

Dowsing or **Diving Rods** - Divination where a forked stick is used to locate water or precious minerals.

Gastromancy - Divination through the form of ventriloquism whereby the voice is lowered to a sepulchral tone and messages are delivered in a trance state.

Geloscopy - Divination from the tone of someone's laughter.

Genethlialogy - Divination by the influence of the stars at birth.

Geomancy - Divination through the study of figures on the ground and the influence of the Earth's "currents".

Graphology - Divination in the analysis of character through handwriting.

Gyromancy - Divination procedure where a person walks in a circle marked with letters until they become dizzy and stumble at different points, thus spelling out a prophesy.

Halolmancy - see Alomancy

Hieromancy or **Hieroscopy** - Divination by observing object of ancient sacrifice.

Hippomancy - Divination from the stamping and neighing of horses.

Horoscopy - Divination through the practice of casting of astrological horoscopes.

Hydromancy - Divination by water including the color, ebb and flow, or ripples produced by pebbles dropped in a pool.

Ichthyomancy - Divination using fish.

Lampadomancy - Divination using lights or torches.

Lecanomancy - Divination using a basin of water.

Libanomancy - Divination using incense and its smoke.

Lithomancy - Divination using precious stones of various colors.

Margaritomancy - Divination by the procedure of using bouncing pearls.

Metagnomy - Divination using visions received in a trance state.

Meteoromancy - Divination from meteors.

Metoposcopy - Divination by the reading of character using the lines if the forehead.

Moleosophy - Divination from the study of moles and indicators of a person's character and future indications.

Molybdomancy - Divination which draws mystic inferences from the hissing of molten lead.

Myomancy - Divination through the study of the prophetic meaning of behavior of rats and mice.

Numerology - Divination by the numerical interpretation of numbers, dates, and the number value of letters.

Oculomancy - Divination from a person's eye.

Oinomancy - Divination using wine.

Oneiromancy - Divination using the interpretation of dreams and their prophetic nature.

Onomancy - Divination through the study of the meaning of names.

Onomantics - Divination where the application of Onomancy is applied to personal names, particularly in the sense of occult interpretation.

Onychomancy - Divination in the study of fingernails.

Oomantia and **Ooscopy** - Divination by using eggs.

Ophiomancy - Divination from serpents.

Orniscopy and **Orinithomancy** - Divination with the study of omens associated with birds, particularly birds in flight.

Ovomancy - Another type of egg divination.

Palmistry - The broad field of divination and interpretation of the lines and structure of the hand.

Pegomancy - Divination that concerns itself with spring water and bubbling fountains and the omens contained therein.

Phrenology - Divination through the long practiced study of head formations.

Phyllorhodomancy - Divination where a person judges the loudness of a rose petal slapped against a hand

Physiognomy - Divination through the study of character analysis through physical features.

Precognition - Divination through an inner knowledge or sense of future events.

Psychography - Divination through a form of mysterious writing having a divinatory nature.

Psychometry - Divination through the faculty of gaining impressions from a physical object and its history.

Pyromancy and **Pyroscopy** - Divination by fire or flame, often assisted by substances thrown onto the flames.

Radiesthesia - Divination with the use of an object. Examples would be a divining rod, Ouija board, automatic, scrying or a pendulum.

Rhabdomancy - Divination using a stick or wand. These methods were used before the divining rod.

Rhapsodomancy - Divination using a book of poetry whereby the book is opened at random and a passage read.

Sciomany - Divination using a spirit guide, a method generally employed by someone channeling.

Scrying - Divination using a crystal, mirrors, bowls of water, ink, or flames to induce visions.

Sideromancy - Divination through the burning of straws with a hot iron, the resulting figures having divinatory properties.

Sortilege - Divination through the casting of lots and the assessment of omens indicated.

Spodomancy - Divination using cinders or soot.

Stichomancy - Divination through another form of throwing open a book and selecting a random passage.

Stolisomancy - Divination that draws omens from the way people dress.

Sycomancy - A form of divination that is performed by writing messages on tree leaves. It is based on the drying process. The slower they dry the better the omen. A similar more modern way is to write on slips of paper and roll them up. In the process one blank paper is included. Then the papers are put in a strainer over boiling water. The first to unroll will be the answer to a posed question

Tasseography - Divination through the reading of tea leaves remaining in the bottom of a finished cup of tea.

Tephramancy - Divination by interpreting the ashes obtained from the burning of tree bark.

Tiromancy - Divination using cheese.

Xylomancy - Divination from pieces of wood. The process involves the shape when collected or the remains after they are burned.

The Symbolism of Crystals

Amber – Good luck stone, helps remove disease and clears negativity and depression.

Agate – Brings forth inspiration from the spiritual realm.

Amethyst – Peace, protection, spirituality, healing, meditation and peaceful sleep.

Angelite – Calms anger, promotes harmony; used in telepathic communication.

Aquamarine – Used to increase psychic power and promote dreams.

Aventurine – Promotes healing, balances the emotions; green aventurine increases perception and promotes prosperity; pink aventurine helps a troubled love life.

Azurite – Promotes mental clarity, and helps clear the subconscious. Helps attune psychic abilities.

Beryl – Promotes and helps psychic abilities.

Black Onyx – Promotes a positive emotional state, and protects against negative energies.

Blue Lace Agate – Promotes health, long life, and grounding. Helps with inspiration.

Calcite – Helps with stress, assists in astral travel, and balances energies. Orange calcite is useful against trauma.

Carnelian – Promotes creative flow. Inspires motivation, courage and confidence.

Celestite – Helps to link with spirit guides and angels.

Chrysocolla – Helps to calm and alleviate fears.

Chrysoprase – Promotes a positive outlook, and attracts success. Promotes spiritual energy.

Citrine – Helps with self esteem, brings about material wellbeing. It prevents nightmares.

Clear Quartz – An aid in meditation, it increases energy and promotes emotional well being.

Diamond – Promotes strength, purity and is a sign of power.

Emerald – Promotes physical healing and is protective in nature.

Fluorite – Aids in focus and concentration. Helps to gather energies and aids in higher self communication. Yellow fluorite promotes self confidence.

Garnet – Increases energies, is an aid in treatment of depression and strengthens relationships.

Haematite – Helps with concentration, memory and self control. It is healing and grounding.

Herkimer Diamond – Helps recall dreams, and releases energy blockages.

Jade – Promotes clarity, wisdom and balances emotion well being. Promotes peaceful sleep and aids in prosperity.

Jasper – One of the most powerful healing stones. Can be used as a talisman.

Jet – Clears negative emotions, calms and helps lift depression. Used to remove negative energies.

Kunzite – Restores balance, and can be used to assist in contacting the higher self. Opens heart and mind.

Kyanite – Clams emotional disorders. Promotes a state of inner peace, works with intuition.

Labradorite – Aids in psychic ability

Lapis Lazuli – Increases will power, awareness and emotional strength.

Malachite – Aids in healing, absorbs negativity, and stimulates creativity.

Moonstone – Used to grant wishes, promotes harmony in relationships, calms emotions and helps with lucid dreaming.

Moss Agate – Helps promote wealth, brings prosperity, establishes connections with Earth spirits, and promotes self confidence.

Obsidian – Protects and assists in grounding. Calms fear and anger, while restoring balance and clarity.

Opal – Helps with insight while attracting inspiration.

Pearl – Promotes clarity, balances emotion and increases confidence and wisdom.

Pyrites – Helps assist in the control of creative thinking.

Red Jasper – Helps to clam and connect with the Earth's energy.

Rhodonite – Promotes patience and selflessness.

Rose Quartz – Helps resolve emotional issues, and restores love.

Ruby – Helps release anger, awakens passion while increasing emotions.

Sapphire – Used for protection, it symbolizes peace and wisdom.

Selenite – Promotes mental focus and clarity. It can be used to assist with clairvoyance.

Smoky Quartz – Promotes self confidence, removes negative influences. Used for grounding and balancing.

Sodalite – Helps calm a troubled mind. Promotes inner peace.

Sugilite – Promotes physical healing and strengthens will. Works to remove impurities from the body. Aids with medication.

Tiger's Eye – Creates a state of harmony and order.

Topaz – Helps remove tension, attracts love and symbolizes light and warmth.

Tourmaline – Helps to protect and ground. It absorbs negativity and brings vitality.

Turquoise – Used for protection and healing. It is used for blessings.

The Symbolism of Birds and Animals

Alligator/Crocodile – Guardian, protector, stealth, ferocity, primal power

Antelope – Vision, foresight, speed, gentleness

Armadillo – Armor, boundaries, protection

Badger – Strength, perseverance, fight, tenacity, prophesy, divination

Bat – Death, rebirth, initiation, transition, change

Bear – Receptive, female energy, earth wisdom, introspection, moon energies

Beaver – Industrious, flexible, creativity

Blackbird – Gatekeeper

Bison (Buffalo) – Wisdom, provider, protector, fertility, sexual vigor, power

Bull – Male, sexual potency, strength, war

Cat – Independence, intuition, female, medicine

Cow – Fertility, prosperity, motherhood, family life

Coyote – Unconditional trust, innocence, playfulness, mischievous, conniving

Crow/ Raven – Change, foresight, prediction, shape shifting, good luck, bad luck, many aspects of witchcraft and magic

Deer – Security, protection, male sexuality, female sexuality, wisdom, storyteller

Dog – Friendship, kindness, loyalty, protection, guardian of ancient secrets

Dolphin/ Porpoise – Understanding, wisdom, unconditional love, laughter, harmony, healing

Dove – Peace, love, marriage, spiritual harmony, purity, clear vision

Dragon – Mythical beast, good luck, energetic, fun-loving, confident

Duck – Love, harmony, domesticity, abundance, motherhood, children, new beginnings

Eagle – Divine, earthy power, freedom, fearlessness, striving for higher goals, clarity, clairvoyance

Fish – Mystery, emotions, lunar magic

Fox – Trickery, guile, secrets, protection, family, maternal instincts

Frog – Cleansing, emotional healing, fertility, change, transformation

Goat – Relaxed, happy-go-lucky, creative, friendly, ambitious

Goose – Storytelling, protection, fertility, rebirth, links with the Goddess

Hare – Fast thinking, intuition, sensitivity, creativity, associated with the moon goddess, fertility

Hawk – The gift of foresight, perception, psychic powers, spirit world messenger, knowledge, wisdom

Heron – Self-reliance

Horse – Freedom, swiftness, stamina, endurance, earthly power, spirit power, strength, self-confidence

Jaguar/ Panther/ Leopard – Visionary, prediction, prophesy, divination, intuition, psychic power

Lion – Strength, majesty, power, leadership

Lizard – Illusions, letting go, adaptability, change, transition

Magpie – Relationships

Moose/ Elk – Strength, endurance, male sexuality, female sexuality, relationships

Monkey – Inquisitive, energetic, competitive, leadership, clever, sharp-witted

Mouse – Attuned sensitivity, messenger, abundance, fertility

Owl – Wisdom, understanding, insight, telepathy, magickal abilities

Ox – Patience, kindness, responsibility, routine, order, discipline

Pig – Diplomacy, common sense, greed

Pigeon – Messages

Rabbit – Fertility, love, fear, cowardice

Ram/ Sheep – Lust, fertility, fool heartiness, youthful zest

Rat – Self-motivated, self-preservation, cheerful, resilience

Robin – New beginnings, protection

Rooster – Flamboyant, communication

Snake – Shedding of the old, transformation, philosophical, mysterious, shrewd, sensual, underworld guardian

Swan – Purity, serenity, peace, spirituality, dignity

Tiger – Rash, impulsive, dynamic, risk-taking, leader
Turtle – Endurance, knowledge, Mother Earth, women

Wolf – Loyalty, freedom, independence, afterlife, rebirth, teacher

Woodpecker – Magic, prophecy, sacred cycles, rain, storms, thunder

Wren – Protection

The Symbolism of Trees, Plants, and Herbs

Angelica – The burning of dried leaves from this tree gives protection and healing

Anise – Used to keep away bad dreams

Apple – Is a symbol of love and friendship, youth, beauty, innocence

Ash – Symbolized by purification and cleansing.

Basil – Protection, repels negativity, brings wealth

Bay – Used as a guardian for homes, protects against illness, burning of its leaves can produce visions.

Beech – Used to represent stability, flow of energy, and it is a protector of knowledge.

Blessed Thistle – Brings wealth and spiritual blessings. Placing it within a room brings strengthening energy.

Cabbage – Brings good luck

Carrot Seed – Used in Vision Quests, brings about visions and journeying.

Catnip – Used to attract happiness and luck, it is also establishes a psychic bond with cats.

Chamomile – Used to relax and aid in meditation. It is also used in prosperity charms.

Chickweed – Used to attract love or maintaining a relationship

Chili – Aids in fidelity and love

Cinnamon – It is an Aphrodisiac and can be used in protection, success and money spells.

Clove – Can be used in banishing spells to rid yourself of hostile or negative energies. Can be used to stop gossip.

Clover – Used for love and fidelity

Coltsfoot – Brings love, wealth and peace

Comfrey – Used for safety when traveling

Cyclamen – Used for love and truth

Dandelion – Strengthens dreams and prophetic power

Dogwood – Used for charm and finesse

Elm – Used for love and purification, symbolized by death and rebirth.

Fennel – Protects against curses

Gardenia – Used for peace and healing

Garlic – Used for magical healing, protection and exorcism

Ginger – Used for success and empowerment

Grape – Used for fertility, garden magic, and attracts money

Hawthorn – A protector of children, a gateway to another world, it symbolizes fertility, happiness and marriage.

Hazel – It is used to make wands, and is a symbol for wisdom, divining and fertility.

Hibiscus – Is used to power divination, promotes dreams and attracts love.

Honeysuckle – It helps in releasing negative feelings about the past and strengthens memory.

Holly – Used in dream magick, courage and wisdom, it is the strongest protective tree.

Hops – Promotes sleep. Used to improve health.

Hyacinth – For love and protection

Hyssop – Used in purification and dispels negativity

Jasmine – Promotes lucid dreams and brings good luck. Promotes friendship and wealth.

Juniper – Calming and promotes good health. Berries can be used to ward off evil.

Lavender – Used for purifying, love and good dreams. It is said to being peace and happiness.

Lemon – Attracts happiness, and is a stress reliever

Lettuce – Induces sleep and is used in divination

Lilly-of-the-valley – Brings peace, harmony and love

Lime – Increases energy, and encourages loyalty

Lotus – Symbol of enlightenment, it elevates and protects

Magnolia – Assures fidelity

Marigold – Renews energy while enhancing visions and dreams

Mistletoe – Used for protection, love and visionary ability. It is hung from the bedpost for good dreams.

Mugwort – Used for clairvoyance, scrying and dream interpretation

Oak – Is associated with divination and prophecy. Grants wisdom, strength and endurance

Olive – Brings peace of mind and faithfulness in love, abundance and sanctuary

Orange – Used to attract peace, power and luck

Orris – Attracts love and romance

Passion Flower – Promotes friendship, brings peace and understanding

Pennyroyal – It increases alertness, and promotes peace between friends and lovers.

Pine – Used for grounding and cleansing, it repels evil. Also used for cleansing and purifying.

Rice – Attracts fertility and money

Rose – Promotes love, generosity and beauty

Rosemary – Used as protection for the home, it also beings mental clarity and sharpens memory.

Rowan – Protects against evil, enchantment and negative energies. Aids in the development of psychic powers.

Sage – It promotes wisdom, fertility, healing and long life.

Silver Birch – Brings new beginnings and healing

Strawberry – Used for love and luck

Sweet Pea – Used for friendship and courage

Thyme – Used for courage and confidence

Tobacco – Bringer of the sacred spirit

Valerian – Promotes love and harmony

Vervain – Used for inner strength and peace

Violet – Used for contentment and love

Willow – Used for healing, love and regenerations. It is also used to empower wishes.

Yew – Used for immortality, transformation and inner wisdom

The Symbolism of Incense and Essential Oils

Acacia (gum arabic) – Protection, promotes psychic awareness

Agarwood (aloes) – Protection, consecration, prosperity, success

Amber – Love, healing

Benzoin – Aids in meditation, grounding, promotes connection with inner self

Bergamot – Attracts success, prosperity, used in rituals of initiation

Camphor – Rebirth, aids in change, transformation, used in lunar magic

Cajeput – Spiritual expansion, freedom

Cedar – Connected with magical power, vitality, immortality

Chamomile – Peace, tranquility, emotional stability, aids in sleep, aids in dreaming

Clary Sage – Aphrodisiac, promotes vivid dreams, encourages dream recall

Clove – Clears the mind, used in past life recall

Copal – Protection, purification, banishing negative energy

Dragon's Blood – Neutralizes negative energy, cleansing, protecting

Eucalyptus – Healing, purifying

Frankincense – Calms the mind, aids in meditation, used in rituals of initiation, used in rites of passage

Galbanum – Clears negativity, used in spells for letting go

Geranium – Balancing, adjusting, assists in new ventures

Helichrysum – Healing, dreams, visions, inspiration

Jasmine – Imagination

Juniper – Clearing negative energies

Lavender – Psychic balance, emotional control

Lemon Grass – Cleansing, purifying, releasing past pain, forgiveness

Mandarin – Inspiration, aids in communication, promotes harmony

Mimosa – Promotes communication with Higher self. Opens a channel for communication with angels and spirit beings

Melissa – Love, harmony, happiness

Musk – Love, sexual attraction

Myrrh – Promotes will power and the courage to follow a soul's path.

Myrtle – Spiritual love, immortality of the soul

Neroli – Love, fertility

Niaouli – Clears negative thoughts, expands consciousness

Nutmeg – Aphrodisiac, clairvoyance, psychic development

Olibanum – Incense of the sun

Palmarosa – For letting go of the past, spiritual illumination

Patchouli – Relaxing aphrodisiac, grounding, promotes the connection with Earth energies

Peppermint – For clarity, courage, increases perception, awareness in the dream state

Ravensara – Spontaneity, determination, deepens meditation

Rose – Strengthens the connection with all aspects of the feminine force

Rosewood – For space clearing

Sandalwood – Aphrodisiac, comforts the dying, opens the gates to spirit guides

Storax – Calming, relaxing, helps unburden the mind

Tea Tree – For space clearing, purification, a light in the darkness

Tobacco – Sacred to Native Americans, usually used for making offerings

Vanilla – Aphrodisiac, attracts love and romance

Vetivert – Protection against negative energies, for over sensitivity to psychic impressions

Ylang Ylang – For love and sensuality

The Symbolism of Colors

Red – Blood, passion, the life essence, power, physical energy, courage, bringing change in difficult circumstances.

Pink – Love and kindness, reconciliation, peace and harmony, compassion, gentle emotions. Associated with family, children and friendship, receptive energy

Orange – Abundance, fertility, heath, joy, attraction, luck, friendship. It marks the boundary between self and others. Associated with the sun, protective energy

Yellow – Communication, the intellect, learning, concentration, also movement, travel and change. It's associated with Mercury, the element of air, the east and protective energy.

Green – The heart and emotions, love, also associated with nature, gardens and growth, money and prosperity, employment. It's also associated with the earth element.

Turquoise – Confidence, inner strength, positive self-esteem; allows expression of wishes.

Blue – Wisdom, patience, possibility, healing the spirit, idealism, truth and justice. It's also associated with the moon, the element of water, the west and reflective energy.

Purple – Royal and priestly, a link with the higher dimension, wisdom, inspiration, magic, religion and spiritual strength. Associated with Osiris, the Egyptian god who judges the dead.

Violet – Temperance, spirituality, repentance, transition from life to death.

Magenta – Letting go, change and transition; moving to a higher plane.

Brown – Associated with earth and earth spirits, instinctive wisdom, the natural world. Use for practical and financial matters, the home, stability, old people, animals. It's also a protective force.

Grey – Compromise and adaptability, psychic protection and secrecy

White – Divinity, potential, the life-force, energy, purity, innocence. Contains all other colors and is associated with the sun.

Black – Death and regeneration. Conclusions that lead to new beginnings, marking a boundary with the past, banishing and releasing negativity, shredding guilt and regret.

Gold – Worldly achievement, wealth, long life and ambition, confidence and understanding. It's also associated with solar deities.

Silver – Dreams, visions, intuition, hidden potential; cosmic intelligence. It's also associated with the moon and lunar deities.

The Symbolism of Gods and Angels

Agni – Hindu god of fire

Amaterasu – Shinto sun goddess

Anael – Archangel of divine love and harmony, beauty and the creative arts

Anubis – Egyptian god of the underworld, depicted with a jackal's head

Aphrodite – Greek goddess of love and beauty; known as Venus to the Romans

Apollo – Greek god of the sun, medicine and music, patron of the Muses

Arianrhod – Celtic mother goddess and keeper of time and fate

Artemis – Greek goddess of the waxing moon, protector of women; known as Diana to the Romans

Bast – Egyptian cat goddess of love and fertility

Brigid – Celtic triple goddess, fire deity and patron of the hearth, healing, prophecy and inspiration

Cassiel – Archangel who assists with overcoming obstacles

Ceridwen – Celtic goddess of wisdom and death; her cauldron contained the brew of inspiration

Cerunnos – The Celtic horned god, like Pan he is a fertility god; god of the witches

Cybele – Phrygian dark moon goddess who governs nature, wild beasts and dark magic

Demeter – Greek goddess of the earth, corn and vegetation; represents abundance and unconditional love; known as Ceres to the Romans

Dhagda – Celtic father god

Dionysus – Greek god and wine and ecstasy; known as Bacchus to the Romans

Epona – Celtic horse-goddess of fertility, abundance and healing

Freya – Norse mother goddess of love, marriage and fertility

Gabriel – Archangel of the moon, associated with the west

Gala – Primeval Greek earth deity, prophetess of Delphi, goddess of wisdom

Ganesha – Elephant-headed Hindu god of wisdom and literature, son of Parvati and Shiva patron business

Hades – Greek go of the underworld; known as Pluto to the Romans

Hathor – Egyptian sky-deity, goddess of love, joy, and dance, usually represented as a cow

Hecate – Greek triple-goddess, rules magic, sorcery, death and the underworld; associated with crossroads

Hermes – Greek messenger god; represents communication, transition and exchange; associated with magic, healing and thieves; known as Mercury to the Romans

Hestia – Greek goddess of the hearth and stability

Horus – Egyptian sun god, depicted with the head of a falcon

Indra – Hindu god of war; associated with weather and fertility

Ishtar – Mesopotamian goddess of sexual love, fertility and war

Isis – Egyptian mother goddess, wife of Osiris and mother of Horus, represents life, loyalty, fertility and magic

Ixchel – Mayan goddess of storms and protector of women in childbirth

Janus – Roman guardian of the entrance and god of transition

Jizo – Japanese protector of children and travelers

Kali – Destructive aspect of the Hindu mother goddess

Kuanyin – Chinese goddess of compassion

Kwannon – Japanese goddess of compassion

Lakshmi – Hindu goddess of abundance, wealth and harmony

Lugh – Celtic sky god, associated with skills and the arts

Luna – Roman goddess of the full moon

Ma'at – Egyptian goddess of truth, justice and order

Mars – Roman god of war, lover of Venus

Manjushri – Buddhist bodhisattva of wisdom

Michael – Archangel of the sun, associated with ruler-ship, marriage and music

Minerva – Roman goddess of wisdom

Mithras – Roman god of light

Morrigan – Celtic goddess of battlefields and death

Nepththys – Sister of Isis, the Egyptian mother goddess, guardian of the dead Osiris

Neptune – Roman god of the sea; known as Poseidon to the Greeks

Odin – Norse sky father god and Master of the Runes

Osiris – Egyptian god of vegetation and judge of the dead, brother and husband of Isis; symbolizes regenerative power of nature

Pan – Greek horned god of wild things, half man, half animal

Parvati – Hindu mother goddess, consort of Shiva

Persephone – Kore, Greek goddess of spring was abducted by Hades and became Persephone, Queen of the underworld

Ra – Egyptian sun god and creator

Raphael – Archangel of the air element, associated with communication and business

Sachiel – Archangel of ruling justice and financial matters

Samael – Protective archangel that helps with matters that require courage or perseverance

Sekhmet – Egyptian goddess of destruction and healing, depicted with the head of a lioness

Selene – Greek goddess of the full moon

Shang Ti – Chinese supreme god

Shiva – Hindu creator god whose meditation sustains the world

Shu – Egyptian god of the air, creator of earth and sky

Sif – Norse goddess of the grasslands, wife of Thor

Sophia – Greek goddess of divine knowledge and wisdom

Sul – Celtic goddess of healing

Sunna – Norse sun goddess

Surya – Hindu sun god

Tara – Tibetan goddess of wisdom and compassion

Thor – Norse god of thunder and industry, married to Sif

Thoth – Egyptian god of wisdom and the moon, scribe of Osiris

Tiamat – Mesopotamian creator goddess

Tsao-chun – Taoist kitchen god

Uriel – Archangel of high magic, and of the earth

Vesta – Roman goddess of the hearth

Vishnu – Hindu protector of the world

Zeus – Greek supreme god; known as Jupiter to the Romans

www.ingramcontent.com/pod-product-compliance
Lightning Source LLC
LaVergne TN
LVHW011720060526
838200LV00051B/2966